Jan Struther

(1901–53) was born Joyce Anstruther. Joyce had a happy child-hood in Buckinghamshire and at school in London. In 1923 she married Anthony Maxtone Graham, a Lloyd's broker and scion of a large and sociable Scottish family. They had three children who were not, she insisted, those portrayed in *Mrs. Miniver*, in spite of similarities of character and incident. During the 1930s Jan Struther became known as the author of stylish poems and essays for *Punch* and Peter Fleming asked her to create a character whose doings would enliven the Court Page of *The Times* – 'an ordinary sort of woman who leads an ordinary sort of life – rather like yourself'. In fact Jan Struther was very far from ordinary: she was tiny, very pretty, and bursting with unconventional zest and enthusiasm (two of her favourite words). The collected articles, which had become enormously popular, were published as *Mrs. Miniver* in 1939, shortly after the outbreak of war. Soon after-wards she went to lecture in America, where *Mrs. Miniver* became a much-loved Hollywood film starring Greer Garson. President Roosevelt told her that it hastened America's entry into the war, and Churchill was to declare that it had done more for the Allies than a flotilla of battleships. This edition includes some wartime letters from Mrs. Miniver to *The Times*, collected and published in book form fo   1953.

Jan Struther

MRS MINIVER

WITH AN INTRODUCTION BY
Valerie Grove

virago

VIRAGO

Published by Virago Press in 1989
Reprinted 1991 (twice), 1992, 2001, 2002, 2008 (twice), 2009, 2011, 2012, 2013

First published in Great Britain by Chatto & Windus 1939
This edition which includes four previously uncollected articles:
'Peace in War'; 'A Moonless Week'; 'Some Points of View',
and 'Time-lag Tragedies' first published 1989

Thanks are due to the Proprietors and Editor of *The Times*, in
which these articles originally appeared, except, 'Mrs. Miniver Makes a List,'
which was first published in *The Queen's Book of the Red Cross*.

A CIP catalogue record for this book
is available from the British Library.

ISBN 978-1-85381-090-9

Typeset in Imprint by M Rules
Printed and bound in Great Britain by
Clays Ltd, St Ives plc

Papers used by Virago are from well-managed forests
and other responsible sources.

MIX
Paper from
responsible sources
FSC
www.fsc.org   FSC® C104740

Virago
An imprint of
Little, Brown Book Group
100 Victoria Embankment
London EC4Y 0DY

An Hachette UK Company
www.hachette.co.uk

www.virago.co.uk

Contents

Letters from Mrs. Miniver to **The Times**
Autumn 1939

Introduction

by Valerie Grove

PEOPLE think they know Mrs. Miniver because they have seen the film, but the real Mrs. Miniver was not Greer Garson: she was equally delightful, but very much more interesting. The real Mrs. Miniver was much more like her creator, Joyce Maxtone Graham, alias 'Jan Struther', writer of poems and witty essays for *Punch*, and mother of three.

Readers may remember that in the film's opening scene, Mrs. Miniver gets off a bus and rushes back to a shop, having had second thoughts about buying an expensive and rather ridiculous hat. This is loosely based on an incident in the book. Mrs. Miniver does dither over buying something. She does get off the bus and scurry through crowded streets to see if it is still for sale. But it isn't a hat, it is an engagement diary in green lizard at 7s. 6d. This is much more characteristic of the real Mrs. Miniver, who rightly feels that a diary has to give pleasure throughout the year. It is one of those trivial objects made momentous by its 'terrible intimacy', and the dull brown calf one she had first chosen for 3s. 9d. would not do. There you have the difference between the character Greer Garson played and the one created by Jan Struther.

Jan Struther was born Joyce Anstruther in 1901. Her mother was Dame Eva Anstruther, a writer made a DBE for her services in sending books to the trenches in World War I; she was known to the family as Granny Dame. Jan's father was Harry Anstruther, Liberal MP for St Andrews Burghs. (It was to avoid confusion with her mother and her mother-in-law, both writers, that J. Anstruther became Jan Struther.)

In her childhood at Whitchurch, Buckinghamshire she drove a pony-and-trap and rode side-saddle; she went to school at Miss Ironside's in London, sharing a classroom with the future Queen Mother, whose pigtails she once dipped in ink. Like her, she was just over five feet tall, and ravishingly pretty, with fine blue eyes. Her son Jamie says men fell in love with her once a month for the whole of her life. She married Anthony Maxtone Graham, a Lloyd's broker, in 1923.

The Maxtone Grahams were an old Scottish family. Every summer, the clan — four families complete with grumbling nannies — gathered at Cultoquhey, the grandparents' huge stone-built pile in Perthshire. There was a lawn tennis court and eleven indoor staff; there was fishing and shooting, and adventures for the children, with tree houses and charades; a family orchestra and dressing up in clothes from the huge dressing-up cupboard on wet days. A typical jape was dressing a realistic dummy figure and seating it on the loo, so that a succession of people open the door and say 'Oh, sorry'.

The children numbered eleven cousins, ten boys and only one girl, Jan's daughter Janet. Just like the children in *Struwwelpeter*, Jan noted: so she wrote *A Modern Struwwelpeter* in the style of Hilaire Belloc's *Cautionary Tales*, one poem about each child — for example, Ruthless Mike and Reckless John, who are beastly to their governess Miss Marlinspike; and Janet, who stares so long at the lovely clothes in the window of Horridge's that she becomes frozen into a wax dummy. The poems appeared in *Punch*, with illustrations by Ernest Shepard, the illustrator of *Winnie-the-Pooh* and *Wind in the Willows*, and were later published in book form, now a rare find.

All Maxtone Graham family gatherings involved evenings of charades and pencil-and-paper games which Jan loved:

Consequences and Clumps and Newspaper Articles and
Weekend Lists, the Dictionary Game, Telegrams and Cruel
Collinses, in which you had to see who could compose the
most politely heartless bread-and-butter letter.

Theirs was (and is still) the kind of family that thrives on
family anecdotes, often centring on aunts. Aunt Elizabeth,
for instance, is known for her malapropisms: 'I must send
some money to the famine in Utopia' and 'Oh, that boy's no
good – he's a real fall-out.' There were five unmarried great-
aunts, a good source of stories. 'At least one daughter in every
generation should remain unmarried,' as Mrs. Miniver
reflects, 'and raise the profession of auntship to a fine art.'

In London Jan lived with her husband and three children
at 16 Wellington Square, just off the King's Road, Chelsea,
not then as fashionable as it is today – it was considered raff-
ish – but instantly recognizable as the neat stucco square in
which the Minivers live. The house had a playroom with a
stage in it, as a garage had been built underneath and formed
a platform, ideal for their amateur dramatics. A photograph
in the family album shows Jan playing the Loch Ness
Monster in 1933.

They also rented the chief coastguard's cottage near Rye in
Sussex for weekends, sometimes leaving the children there
with their nanny while they went off on their adventurous
travels to as yet untouristic places like Majorca and Andorra
and Romania. Although they were often hard up during the
Depression, Jan Struther's motto about travelling was 'Book
now – worry later'.

From this background Jan Struther emerged in the 1930s
as a stylish writer of poems and pieces for *Punch*, *The
Spectator* and *The New Statesman*. In one of her essays she
refers dismissively to herself, 'who never wrote a poem longer
than 30 lines in my life, and miserable puling stuff at that, full
of love and flowers . . .' but in fact she preferred writing
poems and they are crisp, succinct, metropolitan lyrics full of
memorable and pertinent lines on love and loss, youth and

age. 'At a Dull Party' begins: 'In fifty years at most I shall be dead' and ends: 'Then, Christ! what spendthrift folly brought me here – To breathe stale smoke, and drink, talk, think, small beer?'

She was not a novelist; she was happier making keen and accurate observations from everyday life – on a character she has met in the park, on the mysterious fish served for lunch in trains, on how to charm a small child into going to a concert.

Mrs. Miniver was created when Peter Fleming, brother of Ian, asked Jan to brighten up the Court Page of *The Times*: he said it was full of articles about woodpeckers and stoats. Jan was already writing light leaders for *The Times*; he asked her to write about 'an ordinary sort of woman who leads an ordinary sort of life – rather like yourself', although as he must have known, her style of life, her acute perceptions and her talent were all far from ordinary. All these she transferred to the person of Caroline Miniver. ('Miniver' was a name she borrowed from heraldry: it is a kind of white fur used for trimming robes; the name Caroline is teasingly withheld until almost the end of the book.) The pieces appeared every few weeks and were instantly a hit. People would write to Mrs. Miniver; in vain did Jan Struther insist that she was not one and the same, nor were her children the Miniver children. Nobody was fooled. Her children Jamie, Janet and Robert were exactly the same ages as Vin, Judy and Toby, and they did the same things. Jamie remembers that it was he who left his bait to putrefy and cause a ghastly stink as Vin did at 'Starlings'.

Mrs. Miniver was published as a book in October 1939, just after the outbreak of war. Shortly afterwards, Jan took her two younger children to America, where she had been invited to lecture, and her book became a Book of the Month Club choice and a bestseller. These essays, wrote the American poet and author Stephen Vincent Benet (who wrote the line 'Bury my heart at Wounded Knee'), 'are beautifully written, with form, with style and a deceptive simplicity . . .

every word is in place, like the flowers in a beautifully tended garden. *Mrs. Miniver* also manages to project the warmth and wisdom of an engaging personality.' America, still neutral, was charmed by the Minivers, an ordinary British family – so they thought – affected by the war. President Franklin D. Roosevelt told Jan Struther that *Mrs. Miniver* had considerably hastened America's entry into the war; and Winston Churchill said that *Mrs. Miniver* had done more for the Allies than a flotilla of battleships.

In New York they stayed at first in Beckman Place with Aunt Rachel Townsend, who as a matter of course arranged for Jan to be listed in the New York social register; Jan, who had leftward leanings, was not at all pleased. Jan and her children later lived on Central Park South. Robert was sent first to a boys' private school called Trinity School, later the *alma mater* of John McEnroe. 'The reason I have such perfect manners', Robert likes to say, 'is that I went to the same school as John McEnroe.'

Jan bequeathed to her children, says her daughter Janet Rance, the best of all four-letter words: zest. As a child she sometimes wrote her name 'Joyous' instead of Joyce. 'She dashed through life at full tilt, with gaiety, energy and grace. She loved words, and would pause to net and examine them like a butterfly enthusiast.' (Words, as Mrs. Miniver considers, 'were the only net to catch a mood, the only sure weapon against oblivion.')

That zest is apparent from the very first page of *Mrs. Miniver*. Zest for life, she reflects, is 'an accidental gift . . . impossible to acquire, and almost impossible, thank heaven, to lose'. It is lacking in the Lane-Pontifexes, who make her spirits sink every time they ask the Minivers to dinner; but it is there in abundance in Mrs. B, the new charlady, 'with her large good-humoured laugh'.

She would write in longhand, leaning back with her feet up on a sofa, using fine-quality lined paper with a gold-embossed pen. In a lecture entitled 'Pens, Ink and Paper', she said:

'Genius can write on the backs of old envelopes, but mere talent requires the very best stationery that money can buy.' But she was more typically found at some activity:

> One moment she would be learning to play recorders and the theorbo, studying Gaelic or Esperanto, or tackling chess, or baking a hedgehog in clay. A week later she would be making guitars, teaching herself to paper walls or plant-hunting in the Outer Hebrides. She built a boat in the back garden of our cottage near Rye, and we all joined in because her zeal was infectious. If there was ever a dull moment, none of her family or friends can remember it.

She was fond of good practical jokes at all times, although she had two favourite abbreviations, 'J in VBT' (joke in very bad taste) and 'J in WPT' (joke in worst possible taste). Once, to prove that the upper classes never take any notice of their servants, she pretended to be too ill to come down to dinner at Cultoquhey and dressed up as a maid. She served dishes right through the meal and was not recognized by anyone until during the pudding course, when she astonished the company by sitting down on her husband's knee. While in America, she would collect a pocketful of sea-shells from the Atlantic coast, and later scatter them on the Pacific sand with the words 'That'll fox them'.

Jan Struther's name is still familiar today, not just from *Mrs. Miniver* but because of her hymns, particularly the well-loved *Lord of All Hopefulness, Lord of All Joy* – which is sung regularly at weddings and was one of the hymns chosen for the memorial service of the Lockerbie air disaster – and *When a Knight Won His Spurs in the Stories of Old*, a favourite in schools.

She was not at all religious: she was agnostic, and certainly wouldn't dream of going to church unless dragged. But Canon Percy Dearmer, of Westminster Abbey, was asked in 1931 by the Oxford University Press to compile a new hymnbook to rival *Hymns Ancient and Modern*, and he proceeded to ask a few competent versifiers he knew to write a hymn or two. Jan wrote a dozen, proving that although she once said to Percy Dearmer, 'My dear Percy, don't tell me you really believe all this stuff!', she could express her faith in an essentially optimistic universe.

One of her funniest pieces in *Try Anything Twice* (a collection of writings from *Punch* and *The Spectator* published two years before *Mrs. Miniver*, and just as crammed with wisdom and wit) is about going to the fearsome Mrs. Cattermole's establishment to find a new nanny. 'Wanted: A really nice nanny. Born, not made. Must be fond of dogs and able to make toffee. No dragons or duchesses need apply.' In reality, the Maxtone Graham nanny, the spirited Miss Annie Good, was devoted to Jan and stayed until the children were grown up. Jan would not allow her to wear a uniform and they ignored the custom of the nanny calling her charges 'Miss Janet' or 'Master Robert'.

Janet remembers being told to clear up her bedroom, knee-deep in discarded clothes. 'But Mummy,' said Janet, 'you don't tidy your clothes away!' Jan was far too fair-minded to contradict this. 'Well,' she said, 'if I can't be a Shining Example to you, let me at least be a Horrible Warning!'

Despite her upper-class background she was not at all 'respectable and Miniverish' in Janet's view, and quite the reverse of snobbish or stuffy. People who have seen the film assume that she was a twinset-and-pearls type, but this is equally inaccurate about both Miniver and Jan Struther. They share at times a robust exasperation with their social milieu.

Mrs. Miniver writes with distaste of the 'Really Nice Children' in Kensington Gardens: in sleek perambulators, pushed by trained nannies, 'children who had rocking-horses and special furniture with rabbits on, and hats and coats that matched, and grandmothers with houses in the country'. By contrast, in an essay Jan describes the much more appealing children in 'Pump Lane', the slum terrace behind the Square:

these children 'live entirely on jam and white bread but are ravishingly beautiful and unreasonably healthy.'

It is typical of Jan, says her daughter, that she had no great regard for the family jewellery she had inherited. In 1939, when they were leaving London in a hurry, she had just one lunchtime left in which to wrap the jewellery and stow it in a bank. But then she heard that Dame Myra Hess was playing Bach at the National Gallery that lunchtime, and she preferred to go and hear 'Jesu, Joy of Man's Desiring'. 'Bach is so very all-right-making, isn't it?' she said. The family jewellery, left un-banked, was stolen; but all her children inherited her love of music.

Her happy marriage, like so many others, did not survive the effects of the war. Tony Maxtone Graham was with the Eighth Army when he was captured by Rommel and became a prisoner of war, so they did not see each other for five years. After their divorce in 1947 Jan returned to New York and the following year married the love of her life, Adolf Placzek, a tall, erudite Viennese whom she had first met in London in 1938 when he had escaped from Hitler and Jan was helping to look after refugees. 'Dolf' went to America with ten shillings and a suitcase, and eventually became head of the Avery Architectural Library at Columbia University, from which he retired in 1980.

Nobody could fail to be charmed by Mrs. Miniver, who embraces domesticity, parenthood and social life alike with such positive enthusiasm. Even filling a Christmas stocking with tiny things was like writing a sonnet, keeping to the agreeable limitations of a strict form. Mundane things fill her with delight: picking up the blackened twigs from the lopped plane trees in the street, and later watching astonished as they burst into bud in a vase; making conversation with a blimpish colonel at a shooting party: 'Thank God for colonels, thought Mrs. Miniver; sweet creatures, so easily entertained . . . there was nothing in the world so restful as a really good English colonel.'

Mrs. Miniver is launched on the first page as a woman well pleased with her life. She is home again, after the 'irrelevance' of the summer holidays: back to her neat, friendly house in the Square. Tea is already laid in the upstairs drawing-room, where the small fire burns brightly and sun floods through the open windows. She has been buying chrysanthemums. October, she reflects, should be the first month of the year: 'That laborious affair in January was nothing but a name.'

The Minivers' is a world where the eldest son is away at Eton, and they do not even have to make their own early-morning tea. Each morning just before nine, a garage-hand brings the car round to the front door. At weekends they motor down to their country house, 'Starlings', and when the cottage next door is threatened by a developer, they can effortlessly buy that too.

Even if we do not envy Mrs. Miniver the material comfort of her life, we are utterly charmed by the delicate and humorous *aperçus* of her open and fertile mind. 'To be entirely at leisure for one day', she writes, 'is to be for one day an immortal.' Surrounded by domestic servants and therefore not always busy, she is none the less invariably alert. Even a walk on the Embankment throngs her mind with 'glimpses of the sage's vision' – she also wrote a poem about it, called 'Intimations of Immortality in Early Middle Age': feeling at one with every other person in the street, with the thrush and the dray-horse and the cat.

We can trust Mrs. Miniver to see through the absurdity of trying to get Christmas shopping done early. Impossible, she declares. 'The feeling of temporal urgency cannot be artificially induced, any more than the feeling of financial distress. The rich young man who determines to work his way round the world may gain many things, but the experience of poverty is not one of them.' Without the contagious zest of crowds, Christmas shopping in a half-empty shop is 'as joyless as a *mariage de convenance*'.

Such insights enliven everyday life in what might otherwise appear as nugatory as a Mrs. Dale's Diary. Going to the
dentist, choosing a doll with her daughter, embarking on her
first aeroplane flight, driving to Scotland for August: new
perspectives spring to mind. 'She wondered why it had never
occurred to her before that you cannot successfully navigate
the future unless you keep always framed beside it a small
clear image of the past.'

Jan Struther was essentially a sociable creature. But how
one shares Mrs. Miniver's hopes, as she drives down to stay in
the country, that her hosts might happen to share her habits
and 'hate sitting long over meals; walk quickly or not at all;
enjoy arguments, jokes and silences, but detest making conversation; and realize that a day without a chunk or two of
solitude in it is like a cocktail without ice'.

Mrs. Miniver is particularly perceptive on marriage, at its
best a partnership of equal friends. Marriage, she decides, is
like two crescents bound at their points; in the middle there
has to be a leaf-shaped space 'for privacy or understanding,
essential in a happy marriage'. Clem Miniver is a successful
architect whose latest plum is the Vanderhoops' new country
house, and also a thoroughly amenable husband 'who would
generally rather do things than not'. The exasperating thing
about so many of the couples they know, Mrs. Miniver
decides, is their unevenness: 'like those gramophone records
with a superb tune on one side and a negligible fill-up on the
other which you had to take whether you wanted it or not'.

Catching his eye at a dinner party, she reflects: 'It seemed
to her sometimes that the most important thing about marriage was not a home or children or a remedy against sin, but
simply there being always an eye to catch.'

Time and again, the reader is arrested by Mrs. Miniver's
crisp common sense. She happens to enjoy weekend shoots,
loving the winter countryside and the element of 'playing
Indians', but she hates the tedious, cliché-ridden arguments
about whether shooting is right. When asked by the colonel,

at Lady Chervil's table, to give her opinion, she replies that
blood sports are 'indefensible but irresistible', which she
hopes will close the matter. Besides, 'it seemed to her that to
abolish shooting before you had abolished war was like flicking a speck of mud off the top of a midden.'

Mrs. Miniver's children are a touch angelic (there are no
tantrums) but she is perceptive in appraising them – especially Vin's feelings as he goes back to school – and she does
capture the way in which children fill their parents' lives
with rituals. So much of the fun of parenthood lies 'in
watching the children re-make, with delighted wonder, one's
own discoveries'. On Christmas morning, when they burst in
shortly after six to open their stockings: how odd, she
reflects, that the tangerine in the toe of the stocking lingers
even though children get a good supply of fruit all the year
round.

This is one of the moments – when the stockings are being
opened, and the dawn is breaking, and she can hear the distant tinkle of teacups – which Mrs. Miniver feels

> paid off at a single stroke the debit side of parenthood:
> the morning sickness and the quite astonishing pain;
> the pram in the passage, the cold mulish glint in the
> cook's eye; the holiday nurse who had been in the best
> families; the pungent white mice, the shrivelled
> caterpillars; the plasticine on the door-handles . . . the
> alarms and emergencies, the swallowed button, the
> inexplicable earache, the ominous rash appearing on
> the eve of a journey; the school bills and the dentist's
> bills; the shortened step, the tempered pace, the
> emotional compromises, the divided loyalties, the
> adventures continually forsworn.

Here is a glimmer of eternity framed in domesticity.

Over their small enclosed world of routine and contented
pleasures, the threat of war begins to hang like a nimbus. It

starts abruptly with the excursion to get gas-masks, which fills the children with excitement and Mrs. Miniver with the realization of danger. 'It was for this, thought Mrs. Miniver as they walked towards the car, that one had boiled the milk for their bottles, and washed their hands before lunch, and not let them eat with a spoon which had been dropped on the floor.' Gone are her feelings of security and material permanence. 'Look thy last on all things lovely, Every hour . . .' Mrs. Miniver is sustained, as always, by poetry. When the bombing looms, she thinks of things that are truly irreplaceable in the house: like the notches on the nursery doorposts, marking the children's heights.

For the first time we hear Mrs. Miniver express negative feelings: she 'felt she had been wrung out and put through a mangle'. She no longer sees only beauty and falling leaves, but 'allotments and rubbish-tips, the gas-works on one side and a row of dilapidated hoardings on the other'. Suddenly there are spanners in the works of her easeful life. 'Chimneys smoked, pipes burst, vacuum cleaners fused, china and glass fell to pieces, net curtains disintegrated in the wash.' She wakes every day to a mental list of nags: 'Sink plug, ring plumber, get sweep'. At such times, she knew, you must just 'put on spiritual dungarees and remain in them until things are running smoothly again'.

It is this element which adds substance to what would otherwise have been just a charming and amusing period piece. Mrs. Miniver's friends begin to panic about not having achieved what they want in life. She, like everyone else, is rearranging not chrysanthemums, but values. At least the war obliges people to learn new skills, she consoles herself, which bring a freshness and rejuvenation normally alien to most adults, who never learn anything new at all. Deciding, on a whim, to visit the Zoo, she runs into her old friend Professor 'Badger' Badgecumbe, and they go and look at the echidna, a hideous creature who is the incarnation of *accidie*. Inactivity, she decides, is the greatest sin of all.

However long the horror continued, one must not get
to the stage of refusing to think about it. . . . Only by
feeling it to the utmost, and by expressing it, could the
rest of the world help to heal the injury which had
caused it. Money, food, clothing, shelter – people
could give all these and still it would not be enough: it
would not absolve them from the duty of paying in
full, also, the imponderable tribute of grief.

This was the essence of the message to which her American
readers responded. The unfortunate of the world were in lingering torment, while 'the fortunate ones were merely
condemned to watch it from a front seat, unwilling *tricoteuses*
at an execution they were powerless to prevent. The least
they could do was not turn away their eyes . . .'

Finding herself in the Swiss Alps during this anxious last
summer before the war, Mrs. Miniver observes a little
German boy just like Toby. The children of the world are one
nation, she realizes, as are the blind of the world, or the old.
If only governments would spend the price of a few bombers
on free exchange visits for families . . .

But it ought not to NEED a war, she writes to her sister-in-
law, to make people do their duty, talk to each other on buses,
give slum children a holiday in the country, and live simply
and eat sparingly and recover the use of their legs and get up
early enough to see the sun rise. We should seize upon this
mood: press a magic button and retain this vision of ourselves, 'recapture the spirit of this tragic, marvellous and
eye-opening time, so that having recaptured it, we can use it
for better ends'.

Mrs. Miniver, you feel, could rule the world.

Throughout the war Jan Struther continued to write and
to lecture on Anglo-American relations. MGM paid her
handsomely when they made their fanciful film, and with
part of the money she bought two fully equipped ambulances
for the British war effort. A few years later, she refused to see

The Miniver Story, a 1950 sequel even weepier than its pred-
ecessor, in which Greer Garson succumbs to cancer. She
successfully sued MGM for killing off her character, and
rushed in to show Dolf the substantial damages cheque,
crying, 'Oh Dolf, don't let's waste all this lovely money, let's
spend it!' The following year, Jan herself found she had
cancer. She died in the Presbyterian Hospital in New York in
1953 at the age of fifty-two, never having failed in her
courage and good humour, and her ashes were buried at
Whitchurch near Aylesbury, alongside her father.

She had arranged to donate her corneas for transplant, so
that someone else would have a chance to see the beauty of
the world through her eyes; and she had already written her
own epitaph:

> One day my life will end; and lest
> Some whim should prompt you to review it,
> Let her who knows the subject best
> Tell you the shortest way to do it:
> Then say, 'Here lies one doubly blest.'
> Say, 'She was happy.' Say, 'She knew it.'

Postscript
What happened, readers may wonder, to 'Vin, Judy and
Toby', the real Maxtone Graham children? Jamie, the eldest,
is sixty-five and lives by the Tweed, a collector and dealer in
vintage fishing tackle in Peeblesshire and 'having the most
fun I've ever had in my life'. Janet, a magazine writer, married
the monocled Major Patrick Rance, author of the *Great
British Cheese Book* and owner of the most famous cheese
shop in Britain, at Streatley in Berkshire. They have seven
grown-up children and spend a lot of time at their house in
Provence. Robert was born in 1931. After a 'first' at
Cambridge he drifted from the Scots Bar to work as a lawyer
in industry at Sandwich, Kent. When not presiding at public
inquiries into town planning disputes he lives at Sandwich or

at bolt holes in Avignon, Edinburgh or London. He and his wife Claudia own and run two antiques markets. They have a daughter named Ysenda (after one of her great-aunts) who not only looks exactly like her illustrious grandmother but writes wittily for *Harpers & Queen*. Every year Robert, the family archivist, produces a Christmas album for family circulation, full of Maxtone Graham anecdotes and on occasion an essay or two by Jan Struther.

Valerie Grove, London, 1989

Mrs. Miniver Comes Home

I T was lovely, thought Mrs. Miniver, nodding good-bye to the flower-woman and carrying her big sheaf of chrysanthemums down the street with a kind of ceremonious joy, as though it were a cornucopia; it was lovely, this settling down again, this tidying away of the summer into its box, this taking up of the thread of one's life where the holidays (irrelevant interlude) had made one drop it. Not that she didn't enjoy the holidays: but she always felt – and it was, perhaps, the measure of her peculiar happiness – a little relieved when they were over. Her normal life pleased her so well that she was half afraid to step out of its frame in case one day she should find herself unable to get back. The spell might break, the atmosphere be impossible to recapture.

But this time, at any rate, she was safe. There was the house, as neat and friendly as ever, facing her as she turned the corner of the square; its small stucco face as indistinguishable from the others, to a stranger, as a single sheep in a flock, but to her apart, individual, a shade lighter than the house on the left, a shade darker than the house on the right, with one plaster rosette missing from the lintel of the front door and the first-floor balcony almost imperceptibly crooked. And there was the square itself, with the leaves still as thick on the trees as they had been when she left in August; but in August they had hung heavily, a uniform dull green,

whereas now, crisped and brindled by the first few nights of
frost, they had taken on a new, various beauty. Stepping
lightly and quickly down the square, Mrs. Miniver suddenly
understood why she was enjoying the forties so much better
than she had enjoyed the thirties: it was the difference
between August and October, between the heaviness of late
summer and the sparkle of early autumn, between the ending
of an old phase and the beginning of a fresh one.

She reached her doorstep. The key turned sweetly in the
lock. That was the kind of thing one remembered about a
house: not the size of the rooms or the colour of the walls, but
the feel of door-handles and light-switches, the shape and
texture of the banister-rail under one's palm; minute tactual
intimacies, whose resumption was the essence of coming
home.

Upstairs in the drawing-room there was a small bright fire
of logs, yet the sunshine that flooded in through the open
windows had real warmth in it. It was perfect: she felt suspended between summer and winter, savouring the best of
them both. She unwrapped the chrysanthemums and
arranged them in a square glass jar, between herself and the
light, so that the sun shone through them. They were the big
mop-headed kind, burgundy-coloured, with curled petals;
their beauty was noble, architectural; and as for their scent,
she thought as she buried her nose in the nearest of them, it
was a pure distillation of her mood, a quintessence of all that
she found gay and intoxicating and astringent about the
weather, the circumstances, her own age and the season of the
year. Oh, yes, October certainly suited her best. For the
ancients, as she had inescapably learnt at school, it had been
the eighth month; nowadays, officially, it was the tenth: but
for her it was always the first, the real New Year. That laborious affair in January was nothing but a name.

She turned away from the window at last. On her writing-
table lay the letters which had come for her that morning. A
card for a dress-show; a shooting invitation for Clem; two

dinner-parties; three sherry-parties; a highly aperitive notice of some chamber-music concerts; and a letter from Vin at school – would she please send on his umbrella, his camera, and his fountain-pen, which leaked rather? (But even that could not daunt her to-day.)

She rearranged the fire a little, mostly for the pleasure of handling the fluted steel poker, and then sat down by it. Tea was already laid: there were honey sandwiches, brandy-snaps, and small ratafia biscuits; and there would, she knew, be crumpets. Three new library books lay virginally on the fender-stool, their bright paper wrappers unsullied by subscriber's hand. The clock on the mantelpiece chimed, very softly and precisely, five times. A tug hooted from the river. A sudden breeze brought the sharp tang of a bonfire in at the window. The jig-saw was almost complete, but there was still one piece missing. And then, from the other end of the square, came the familiar sound of the Wednesday barrel-organ, playing, with a hundred apocryphal trills and arpeggios, the 'Blue Danube' waltz. And Mrs. Miniver, with a little sigh of contentment, rang for tea.

The New Car

M<small>RS.</small> Miniver woke up one morning with a sense of
doom, a knowledge that the day contained something
to be dreaded. It was not a crushing weight, such as an oper-
ation, or seeing one's best friend off to live in Tasmania; nor
was it anything so light as a committee meeting, or a deaf
uncle to tea: it was a kind of welter-weight doom.

At first it puzzled her. So far as she knew, she had no
appointments that day, either pleasant or unpleasant, and that
in itself was good. *To be entirely at leisure for one day is to be
for one day an immortal*: according to the Chinese proverb
she ought to have been feeling god-like. But the small, dull
weight continued to drag and nag.

Clem put his head in, dishevelled from a bath. Not for the
first time, she felt thankful that she had married a man whose
face in the ensuing sixteen years had tended to become sardonic rather than sleek. It was difficult to tell, when people
were young and their cheek-lines were still pencilled and deli-
ble. Those beautiful long lean young men so often filled out
into stage churchwardens at forty-five. But she had been lucky,
or had a flair; Clem's good looks were wearing well. The great
thing, perhaps, was not to be too successful too young.

At the moment his expression was anything but sardonic.

'She ought to be here by nine,' he said eagerly, and van-
ished.

Mrs. Miniver remembered with a bump, felt dismayed, knew that her dismay was unreasonable, and tried to argue it out of existence. A new car was a thing to be pleased over; it was high time they had one. The old Leadbetter had got to the stage when nothing less than an expensive overhaul would do any good; it had developed sinister fumes, elusive noises, incurable draughts; it was tiring for Clem on his long drives. And a week ago, when Clem, straight from the Motor Show, had spent the whole evening musing happily over catalogues, she had realized that the game was up. Her usual attitude – that they didn't really need a new car – was plainly untenable, and this time she could not even fall back upon a plea for economy. They could perfectly well afford it now. Clem's plans for the new building estate had gone through; and there was the Vanderhoops' country house as well – a plum. Besides, this scene had been replayed, with variations, many times, and they both knew that the basis of her invariable reluctance about new cars was not thrift but sentiment. She simply could not endure the moment when the old one was driven away.

Mrs. Miniver was a fool about inanimate objects. She had once bid furiously at an auction for a lot described as 'Twelve kitchen chairs; also a small wicker knife-basket.' Clem, knowing the size of their kitchen, made urgent signals to her across the room. She stopped bidding, and the lot was knocked down to someone else for more than its value by a grateful but mystified auctioneer.

'You got mixed up in the lot numbers, didn't you?' Clem said afterwards.

'No,' she said, guiltily. 'I'm awfully sorry. It was that knife-basket. I suddenly thought – so wretched not to be grand enough to be in a lot by itself. Just tagged on to kitchen chairs like that. Clem – a *small* wicker knife-basket. . . .'

As for cars, they were in a class apart, somewhere between furniture and dogs. It wasn't, with her, a question of the pathetic fallacy. She did not pretend to herself that cars had souls or even minds (though anybody, seeing the difference that can exist between one mass-produced car and another, might be excused for believing that they have at least some embryonic form of temperament). No, it was simply a matter of *mise en scène*. A car, nowadays, was such an integral part of one's life, provided the aural and visual accompaniment to so many of one's thoughts, feelings, conversations, decisions, that it had acquired at least the status of a room in one's house. To part from it, whatever its faults, was to lose a familiar piece of background.

She got up and turned on her bath. Even through the rushing of the water she could hear the old Leadbetter coming down the square: a garage-hand brought it round every morning just before nine. She listened for the gear-change as it picked up speed after the corner, then for the squeal of the brake, the stopping of the engine, the slamming of the door, the man's footsteps receding up the square. It was really ridiculous, she thought, to mind so much; and gave herself an extra handful of bath-salts as a futile antidote to woe. Almost at once there was the sound of another car drawing up, a smooth virile purring, the discreet opening and closing of a solid well-fitting door. Then Clem's voice in the square and Judy's feet jigging on the pavement. It was intolerable. Old horses one pensioned off in a paddock, where one could go and see them occasionally. Or one even allowed them to pull the mowing-machine in round leather boots. But this part-exchange business—

Judy came racing upstairs and hammered on the door, shrill with excitement.

'Mummy! The new car's come!'

'Lovely,' called Mrs. Miniver.

'And I've been helping Daddy clear the maps and things out of the old one before they drive it away.'

Heavens, how relentlessly children dotted the i's!

'Run along,' called Mrs. Miniver. 'I'll be down quite soon.'

She turned both the taps full on again, put a thick lather of soap over her ears, and began to sing, noisily.

Guy Fawkes' Day

THEY didn't take the children down to Starlings much in the winter, until the Christmas holidays. When the days were short a week-end was scarcely worth while. They made an exception, however, for Guy Fawkes' Day, that kindly and prescient spirit having planned his crime to coincide – or as nearly as makes no difference – with the autumn half-term.

The Miniver family had a passion for fireworks; and a fire-works display in a small London garden is an emasculate thing, hampered at every turn by such considerations as the neighbours, the police, and the fragility of glass and slate. So on Saturday morning they picked up Vin at Eton and drove across country to Starlings. Mrs. Miniver was relieved to find that public school had not made him too grand to enjoy play-ing road competitions with the two younger children. He was, like his father, a timeless person, uninfluenced by his own age and unconscious of other people's. Judy was quite different. She was as typically nine now as she had been typically six, and three. Age, to her, was an important and exciting quality: she was never quite at ease with other children until she had asked them how old they were. As for Toby, he remained, in this as in most other matters, unfathomable.

In childhood the daylight always fails too soon – except when there are going to be fireworks; and then the sun dawdles

intolerably on the threshold like a tedious guest. There were
no clouds that day, and even after sunset the western sky
remained obstinately full of pearl-grey light. It was not so
bad for Vin, who was helping his father to pin Catherine-
wheels on to the fence and to prop up rocket-sticks in bottles
on the lawn; but Judy and Toby, their noses pressed against
the inside of the window-panes, were rampant with impa-
tience long before Clem decided that darkness had officially
fallen and the show could begin.

Swathed in coats and scarves, they went out and sat in a
row on the little flagged terrace. The evening might have
been ordered with the fireworks; it was cold, still, and
starry, with a commendable absence of moon. And when
the first rocket went up Mrs. Miniver felt the customary
pricking in her throat and knew that once again the
enchantment was going to work. Some things – conjurers,
ventriloquists, pantomimes – she enjoyed vicariously, by
watching the children's enjoyment; but fireworks had for
her a direct and magical appeal. Their attraction was more
complex than that of any other form of art. They had pattern and sequence, colour and sound, brilliance and
mobility; they had suspense, surprise, and a faint hint of
danger; above all, they had the supreme quality of transience,
which puts the keenest edge on beauty and makes it touch
some spring in the heart which more enduring excellences
cannot reach.

It was certainly the best display they had ever had. Mrs.
Miniver herself, when buying fireworks, was apt to be led
away by fantastic titles; she would order Humming Spiders,
Witches' Cauldrons, Mines with Serpents, Bouquets of
Herbes, and Devils among the Tailors, largely in order to see
what they were like. But Clem knew that with fireworks, as
with cocktails, the sober, familiar names usually produced the
most interesting results. He laid out a certain amount on
Roman Candles, Catherine-wheels, and Tourbillions, but for
the most part he rightly concentrated on rockets.

There was one bursting now, a delicate constellation of many-coloured stars which drifted down and lingered in the still air. Watching it, she thought that of all the arts this was the one which showed the greatest contrast between the raw materials and the finished work. Words, pigments, notes of music – all of these, unmarshalled, possessed a certain beauty of their own; a block of marble had at least an imaginable relationship with the statue which it was to become; stone, brick, and concrete, Clem's materials, did not seem impossibly remote from the houses which he would make of them. But this fiery architecture, these fragments of luminous music, these bright, dream-like, and impermanent pictures in the sky – what had they to do with nitre, sulphur and charcoal, with gummed paper, cotton-wick, and a handful of mineral salts?

The show was nearly over. Vin and his father were letting off the last few rockets. Their faces, occasionally lit up, were absorbed, triumphant, serene. Judy was shivering with cold and excitement. Toby, his feet sticking out over the edge of the seat, was completely immobile, but whether from profound emotion or too many coats it was impossible to tell. As for Mrs. Miniver, she was having a race with time. Some half-remembered words had been haunting her all the evening, a line of poetry, perhaps, or an old saying, something about brightness, something exquisitely appropriate. 'Brightness . . .' What was it? The rest of the phrase eluded her, though she felt the rhythm of it; and she knew that she must remember it before the fireworks were finished, or it would be no use.

The final rocket went up, a really large one, a piece of reckless extravagance. Its sibilant uprush was impressive, dragonlike; it soared twice as high as any they had had before; and the moment it had burst, Mrs. Miniver remembered. 'Brightness falls from the air' – that was it! The sparks from the rocket came pouring down the sky in a slow golden cascade, vanishing one by one into a lake of darkness.

> Beauty is but a flower
> Which wrinkles will devour;
> Brightness falls from the air;
> Queens have died young and fair;
> Dust hath closed Helen's eye—

It was quite irrelevant, really, a lament by Nashe in time of
pestilence, nothing to do with fireworks at all. But she knew
that it was just what she had needed to round off the scene for
her and to make its memory enduring. Words were the only
net to catch a mood, the only sure weapon against oblivion.

The Eve of the Shoot

EVERY year without fail Mrs. Miniver received an invitation written in a sloping Victorian hand on lavishly stout cream-laid. The right-hand top corner was embossed in heavy black Gothic with the address 'Chervil Court, Crampton.' On the left were three tiny formalized sketches – a telegraph-pole, an upright telephone, and a railway engine of the Stephenson period, stocky and high-funnelled – followed respectively by the words, 'Great Yettingford,' 'Buntisley 3,' and 'Slape Junction.' The letter began with old Lady Chervil's unvarying formula:

My dear Mrs. Miniver,

Chervil and I shall be delighted if you and your Husband will stay with us from Friday 19th to Monday 22nd November.

(She would have gone to the guillotine sooner than use the expression 'week-end.')

Mrs. Miniver tossed the letter over to Clem. There must, he remarked, be an air-port near there by now, and sketched in under the other pictures a little pre-War biplane, single-engined and very short in the wing, followed by the words, 'Market Bumbleton.' There was no need for them to discuss whether they were going to accept the invitation. They always

went to Chervil. The shooting was excellent, the food beyond
praise; and it was soothing, for a short time, to slow oneself
down to the pace of its old-fashioned ritual, and to spend
three days in inverted commas.

'And what,' said the Colonel, turning to Mrs. Miniver at
dinner on the night of their arrival, 'is your opinion . . .?'

She had been afraid of this ever since, over the vol-au-
vent, that woman in the wrong shade of green, on being asked
whether she was coming out with the guns to-morrow, had
shut her eyes and ever so delicately shuddered: thus plunging
everybody around her into what was bound in that company
to be a tedious and unprofitable discussion. Tedious because
neither side possessed any currency but clichés, and unprofitable because it was clear from the outset that neither side
was going to budge an inch. Besides, what a hare to start at a
shooting-party! You might with as much sense and propriety
get up at a Lord Mayor's banquet and give a harangue on
vegetarianism. If you felt as strongly as that, the only thing to
do was to have 'flu and stay away.

It raged, if such a stale controversy could be said to rage,
all through the quail, the ice-pudding, and the mushrooms on
toast. Well-worn coins rang in Mrs. Miniver's ears. 'After all,
the birds get a sportin' chance. . . .' 'Animals may not have
souls, but still . . .' 'Now take huntin' . . .' 'Oh, *bull*-fightin' –
that's *quite* a different kettle of fish. . . .' Italics bred italics.
Dropped g's fell as thick as confetti. Sooner or later the tide of
argument was almost certain to reach her end of the table, but
she made up her mind that she would not be drawn in. She
had been through it all too many times before, and even in
circles where one could speak freely the subject had become
too hackneyed to be borne. Her own attitude, she knew, was
unethical but honest. She did not happen to be personally
squeamish, which was merely a matter of chance. She
enjoyed any display of skill; she enjoyed bare trees, rimy pastures, breath made visible by frost, the smell of dead leaves,

and the intricate detail of winter hedgerows; above all, she enjoyed that element of woodcraft, that sense of 'playing Indians,' which games fail to supply and which the detractors of hunting, shooting, and fishing so often mistake for blood-lust. And although she admitted that all shooting was cruel and that all cruelty was wrong, it seemed to her that to abolish shooting before you had abolished war was like flicking a speck of mud off the top of a midden.

For the moment the conversation on either side of her had flowed away, leaving her on a blessed little island of peace and silence. She had time to study the heraldic beauty of the pineapple (for they had now reached dessert), to speculate on the second footman's private life (he had a studious, enigmatic face and probably read philosophy), and to reflect how unpleasing, musically, is the sound of a pack of upper-class English voices in full cry.

Lady Chervil, however, was a watchful and tidy-minded hostess of the old school, who regarded a dinner-party as a quadrille and disapproved of islands. With a masterly verbal tweak she readjusted the guests who had got out of step. 'And what,' said the Colonel, turning to Mrs. Miniver, 'is *your* opinion of all these blood sports?'

'I think they are indefensible, but irresistible,' she answered. She had found through long experience that this remark usually closed the subject pretty quickly. It left very little to be said. Besides, she meant it.

'Ha!' said the Colonel. She noted with delight that he really did say 'Ha!' This made a valuable addition to her collection. She had lately acquired a 'Humph!' and two 'Whews!' but she was still waiting in vain for a 'Pshaw!'

'Tell me,' she said, 'weren't you with an uncle of mine in Singapore – Torquil Piggott?'

'*Piggy!*' exclaimed the Colonel, beaming gratefully, and plunged into reminiscence. Thank God for colonels, thought Mrs. Miniver; sweet creatures, so easily entertained, so biddably diverted from senseless controversy into comfortable monologue: there was nothing in the world so restful as a really good English colonel. She nailed her smile to the mast and reverted to the pineapple and the second footman. Clem caught her eye across the table. It seemed to her sometimes that the most important thing about marriage was not a home or children or a remedy against sin, but simply there being always an eye to catch.

Christmas Shopping

ONE of the minor arts of life, thought Mrs. Miniver at the end of a long day's Christmas shopping, was the conservation of energy in the matter of swing doors. With patience and skilful timing it was very seldom necessary to use your strength on them. You could nearly always follow close behind some masterful person who had already done the pushing; and if you were too late for that and the door had begun to swing towards you, then it was well worth pausing for a second until it swung away again and needed only a gentle encouragement. This seemed obvious enough; but there was an astounding number of people who seemed to glory in taking the line of most resistance, hurling themselves against an approaching door and reversing its direction by brute force, as though there were virtue in the act. They must lead, she reflected, very uncomfortable lives.

Placing herself neatly in the wake of a bull-necked woman in tweeds, she slipped out of the shop. There was a raw wind; sleety rain was beginning to fall, blurring the lamplight; the pavements were seal-sleek; it was settling down into one of those nasty wet evenings which the exiled Londoner longs for with a quite unbearable nostalgia.

She tumbled all her parcels into the back of the car, slid, happy but exhausted, into the driving-seat, and set off for home. The double screen-wiper wagged companionably, uttering over and over again the same faint wheedling word, which she could never quite make out. It was a dissyllable, something like 'receive' or 'bequeath.' She was glad, at any rate, that they now had a screen-wiper which moved at a constant speed. Their last had been one of those which work off the induction: lively and loquacious when you are at a standstill, sulky and slow as soon as you get going and really need its help – like the very worst type of human being.

She felt a little guilty: it was the first time she had caught herself comparing the beloved old car unfavourably in any way with the usurping new one.

Getting home was evidently going to be a long job. The usual six o'clock home-going stream was in spate with Christmas crowds, and Oxford Street was a solid jam. It was her own fault, she had to admit, as she sat back and waited for the lights to change. Every year the same thing happened. At the beginning of November she made up her mind that this time, for once, she would get her Christmas shopping done early. She went as far as writing out a list – and there, for several weeks, the matter rested. At intervals she tried to pretend that Christmas Day fell on the 5th of December, or, alternatively, that all her friends and relations lived in South Africa and that she had to catch an early mail; but it was no use. The feeling of temporal urgency cannot be artificially produced, any more than the feeling of financial distress. The rich young man who determines to work his way round the world may gain many things, but the experience of poverty is not one of them. He knows that in the ultimate emergency he can always cable home for funds; and Mrs. Miniver knew perfectly well that Christmas was not until the 25th of December, and that all the people on her list lived in England.

(The screen-wiper wagged steadily. 'Sea-green . . . sea-green . . .' Perhaps that was nearer the mark?)

Besides, successful present-choosing depends very largely upon the right atmosphere, upon the contagious zest of crowds, upon sudden inspirations and perceptions, heightened rather than otherwise by a certain sense of pressure in space and time. To do it cold-bloodedly, in a half-empty shop, without any difficulty or competition, is as joyless as a *mariage de convenance*. So perhaps it was just as well, she told herself consolingly, that she had, as usual, left it till the middle of December.

('Wee Free . . . Wee Free . . .' Warmer. She'd get it yet.)

The lights changed. She put the car into bottom gear, paused, then let in the clutch. It occurred to her as she did so that it was not only people's physical reactions to those three colours that had become automatic but their mental ones as well. Red, yellow, green – frustration, hope, joy: a brand-new conditioned reflex. Give it a few more years to get established, and psychiatrists would be using coloured rays, projected in that sequence, for the treatment of melancholia; and to future generations green would no longer suggest envy, but freedom. In such haphazard ways are symbolisms born and reborn.

At the next crossing, red again. Frustration – but somehow one accepted it without resentment, simply because it was not imposed by a human hand. One could be annoyed with a policeman, but not with a tin hollyhock. The same was true of automatic telephones: ever since the dialling system had come in the world's output of irritation must have been halved. It was an argument for the mechanization of life which had not previously struck her.

She got home at last. Clem was already in, with his legs stretched out in front of the fire.

'Successful?' he asked, seeing her festooned with parcels.

'Look here,' she said, 'that screen-wiper – I *think* what it says is "Beef Tea."'

'My goodness,' said Clem. 'I believe you're right.'

Three Stockings

HOWEVER much one groaned about it beforehand, however much one hated making arrangements and doing up parcels and ordering several days' meals in advance – when it actually happened Christmas Day was always fun.

It began in the same way every year: the handle of her bedroom door being turned just loudly enough to wake her up, but softly enough not to count as waking her up on purpose; Toby glimmering like a moth in the dark doorway, clutching a nobbly Christmas stocking in one hand and holding up his pyjama trousers with the other. (He insisted upon pyjamas, but he had not yet outgrown his sleeping-suit figure.)

'Toby! It's only just after six. I did say not till seven.'

'But, Mummy, I can't tell the time.' He was barefoot and shivering, and his eyes were like stars.

'Come here and get warm, you little *goat*.' He was into her bed in a flash, stocking and all. The tail of a clockwork dog scratched her shoulder. A few moments later another head appeared round the door, a little higher up.

'Judy, darling, it's *too* early, honestly.'

'I know, but I heard Toby come in, so I knew you must be awake.'

'All right, you can come into bed, but you've got to keep quiet for a bit. Daddy's still asleep.'

And then a third head, higher up still, and Vin's voice, even deeper than it had been at Long Leave.

'I say, are the others in here? I thought I heard them.'

He curled himself up on the foot of his father's bed. And by that time, of course, Clem was awake too. The old transparent stratagem had worked to perfection once more: there was nothing for it but to switch on the lights, shut the windows, and admit that Christmas Day had insidiously but definitely begun.

The three right hands – Vin's strong and broad, Judy's thin and flexible, Toby's still a star-fish – plunged in and out of the three distorted stockings, until there was nothing left but the time-hallowed tangerine in the toe. (It was curious how that tradition lingered, even nowadays when children had a good supply of fruit all the year round.) Their methods were as different as their hands. Vin, with little grunts of approval, examined each object carefully as he drew it out, exploring all its possibilities before he went on to the next. Judy, talking the whole time, pulled all her treasures out in a heap, took a quick glance at them and went straight for the one she liked best – a minikin black baby in a wicker cradle. Toby pulled all his out, too, but he arranged them in a neat pattern on the eiderdown and looked at them for a long time in complete silence. Then he picked up one of them – a big glass marble with coloured squirls inside – and put it by itself a little way off. After that he played with the other toys, appreciatively enough; but from time to time his eyes would stray towards the glass marble, as though to make sure it was still waiting for him.

Mrs. Miniver watched him with a mixture of delight and misgiving. It was her own favourite approach to life: but the trouble was that sometimes the marble rolled away. Judy's was safer; Vin's, on the whole, the wisest of the three.

To the banquet of real presents which was waiting downstairs, covered with a red and white dust-sheet, the stocking-toys, of course, were only an *apéritif*; but they had a

special and exciting quality of their own. Perhaps it was the
atmosphere in which they were opened – the chill, the black
window-panes, the unfamiliar hour; perhaps it was the powerful charm of the miniature, of toy toys, of smallness
squared; perhaps it was the sense of limitation within a strict
form, which gives to both the filler and the emptier of a
Christmas stocking something of the same enjoyment which
is experienced by the writer and the reader of a sonnet; or
perhaps it was merely that the spell of the old legend still per-
sisted, even though for everybody in the room except Toby
the legend itself was outworn.

There were cross-currents of pleasure, too: smiling glances
exchanged by her and Vin about the two younger children
(she remembered suddenly, having been an eldest child, the
unsurpassable sense of grandeur that such glances gave one);
and by her and Clem, because they were both grown-ups;
and by her and Judy, because they were both women; and by
her and Toby, because they were both the kind that leaves the
glass marble till the end. The room was laced with an invisible network of affectionate understanding.

This was one of the moments, thought Mrs. Miniver,
which paid off at a single stroke all the accumulations on the
debit side of parenthood: the morning sickness and the quite
astonishing pain; the pram in the passage, the cold mulish
glint in the cook's eye; the holiday nurse who had been in the
best families; the pungent white mice, the shrivelled caterpil-
lars; the plasticine on the door-handles, the face-flannels in
the bathroom, the nameless horrors down the crevices of
armchairs; the alarms and emergencies, the swallowed button,
the inexplicable earache, the ominous rash appearing on the
eve of a journey; the school bills and the dentists' bills; the
shortened step, the tempered pace, the emotional compro-
mises, the divided loyalties, the adventures continually
forsworn.

And now Vin was eating his tangerine, pig by pig; Judy
had undressed the black baby and was putting on its frock

again back to front; Toby was turning the glass marble round and round against the light, trying to count the squirls. There were sounds of movement in the house; they were within measurable distance of the blessed chink of early morning tea. Mrs. Miniver looked towards the window. The dark sky had already paled a little in its frame of cherry-pink chintz. Eternity framed in domesticity. Never mind. One had to frame it in something, to see it at all.

The New Engagement Book

TWELFTH Night was over; the decorations were down; Christmas (which, like all extremes, dates easily) seemed as *démodé* as a hat in a passport photograph: and still Mrs. Miniver had not bought herself a new engagement book, but was scribbling untidy notes on the fly-leaf of the old one.

As usual, she had meant to buy one before leaving London for Starlings; but as usual, there hadn't been time. It is a thing, she knew, which must never be done in a hurry. An engagement book is the most important of all those small adjuncts to life, that tribe of humble familiars which jog along beside one from year's end to year's end, apparently trivial, but momentous by reason of their terrible intimacy. A sponge, a comb, a tooth-brush, a spectacle-case, a fountain-pen – these are the things which need to be chosen with care. They become, in time, so much a part of one that they can scarcely be classed as inanimate. Insensitive, certainly – but so are one's nails and hair. And although some of them can be given away if one takes a dislike to them, with others the only remedy is destruction; and there is no case on record of anybody, however rich, being strong-minded enough to throw an almost new sponge into the fire. Meekly, one puts up with its inconvenient shape, its repulsive texture, and the cretinous face which is discernible among its contours when it is lightly squeezed. Eventually, thank goodness, it will wear out; or with any luck one may leave it behind in an hotel.

But an engagement book, once used, is a far worse problem. To give it away is impossible, to lose it is disastrous, and to scrap it and start a new one entails a laborious copying out of all the entries that have already been made. Unless, of course, one is prepared to leave the first part of the new book blank and risk giving one's biographers – if any – the impression that one has suffered from a prolonged attack of leprosy. Or worse.

So it wasn't until well into January that Mrs. Miniver, up for the day from Starlings to go to the dentist, found herself in a stationer's shop with enough leisure to give the matter the attention it deserved. She stopped in front of the rack marked 'Diaries' and prepared to enjoy herself.

The first book she picked up was bound in scarlet morocco. Rather nice; but it turned out to be one of those unnatural affairs which show two weeks at an opening. A fortnight, she always felt, was an impossible division of time, relevant neither to God's arrangements nor to man's. Days were the units which mattered most, being divided from each other by the astounding phenomenon of losing and regaining consciousness. (How brave, how trustful people are, to dare to go to sleep!) But a day at an opening was no good – too much for an engagement book, not enough for a real diary. A week was what she wanted: a nice manageable chunk of time with a beginning, a middle, and an end, containing, if desired, a space for each of the wonders of the world, the champions of Christendom, the deadly sins, or the colours of the rainbow. (Monday was definitely yellow, Thursday a dull indigo, Friday violet. About the others she didn't feel so strongly.)

Of the week-at-an-opening kind, there were only three left. That was the worst of leaving it so late. One was bound in crimson leatherette, one in brown calf, and one in green lizard-skin. She rejected the leatherette at once. In a spasm of post-Christmas economy, she had once bought a very cheap engagement book, and it had annoyed her for twelve months; everything she put down in it looked squalid. The green lizard, on the other hand, was marked seven-and-sixpence, which seemed a fabulous price to pay. She decided on the brown calf, at three-and-nine: a smooth, pleasant little volume, an honest and sturdy companion for a year's march. It would wear well; she could not possibly, she knew, take a dislike to it. She paid, put it into her bag, left the shop and stepped on to a No. 11 bus. She would catch the train back to Starlings with twenty minutes to spare.

Half-way down the Pimlico Road she suddenly pressed the button and jumped off the bus.

'Forgotten something,' she said, smiling apologetically at the conductor. There was no other bus in sight, so she walked back to Sloane Square as fast as she could. At this very moment, perhaps, the green lizard-skin diary was being bought by somebody else – some wholly unsuitable person who merely wanted to get one in a hurry; a rich, earnest woman who would fill it with committee meetings, or a business man who would not even glance at the binding when he opened it to jot down the words 'Dine George.' While she herself, with all her dearest activities soberly confined in brown calf, would be thinking about it in an agony of regret.

But it was still there. She produced another three-and-nine-pence and bore it away delighted. After all, the difference was very little more than the price of a taxi. (But she had to take a taxi to Charing Cross as well.)

In the train she pulled out the little green shining book and entered in it, from memory, the few and simple appointments which the year had so far contained. 'Meet Clem, 2.27.' 'Pike-fishing with Vin.' 'Lunch Bucklands.' 'Bridget for week-end.' Bare and laconic; yet those first days had been crammed, like all other days, with feelings, ideas and discoveries. And so it would go on until the book was complete – a skeleton map of her year, which to anybody else's eye would convey no picture whatever of her mental landscape. But she, glancing through it twelve months hence, would be able to fill in many, though not all, of the details; how, on the way out from the station, Clem had told her about the new Gloucestershire job; how she and Vin had seen a heron; how the Bucklands had given them home-cured gammon with pickled peaches; and Bridget's fascinating story about her cousin, the threepenny-bit, and the deaf chimney-sweep.

The Last Day
of the Holidays

THE last day of the holidays dawned relentlessly wet. The last day down at Starlings, that is, which for Vin was what counted. Judy liked London equally well, and Toby lived in a landscape of his own; but for Vin the twenty-four hours in London on his way back to school were only a kind of twilight, with one foot already in the grave. There was always some treat to mitigate it – the circus, a theatre, or a music-hall; but even this, enjoyable as it was, had a tinge of the macabre in its glory, like the pomps and splendours of a funeral feast.

Not that he disliked school; but it had to be regarded, he found, as another life, to be approached only by way of the Styx. You died on the station platform, were reborn, not without pangs, in the train, and emerged at the other end a different person, with a different language, a different outlook, and a different scale of values. That was what the stray grown-ups you met in the holidays did not seem to understand when they asked you the fatuous and invariable question, 'How do you like school?' It was impossible to answer this properly, because the person of whom they asked it never, strictly speaking, arrived at school at all.

The reverse process – getting back into his home skin – though not in the least painful, was almost as difficult. For one thing, he had always outgrown it a little, and, like his home clothes, it had to be adjusted. Sometimes, before it was a comfortable fit, nearly a week had gone by; he was almost half-way to the half-way mark – that significant water-shed beyond which the days raced downhill in a heartless torrent.

However full the children packed them, however early they got up, however late, by various ruses, they contrived to go to bed, the holidays were always far too short. There was never time to carry out more than three-quarters of the plans they made. Some of these – such as building a tree-hut or explor- ing the mill-stream to its source – never got started at all; others they had to leave half done, such as the cardboard castle which had been lurking for two years in a corner of the boxroom, roofless, but with a practicable portcullis. Somehow it never seemed possible to finish things like that during the next holidays. There was always some newer craze.

This time their main occupation had been fitting up one of the outhouses like the cabin of a ship, with built-in bunks, straw palliasses, and a locker full of imaginary charts. (Vin drew the charts, Judy painted them, and Toby put in the casual dolphins.) But they had also made a brick-kiln in the kitchen garden and baked in it at least a dozen quite satisfac- tory bricks. Not enough to build anything with, it is true, but enough to give them a reassuring feeling that if they were ever wrecked on a desert island they would soon be able to run up a house or two: always provided, of course, that the island had a clay soil. And they had dammed the stream, and undammed it again; and watched the woodmen cutting and splitting young chestnuts for palings; and watched the blacksmith, and the wheelwright, and the man who came to mend the roof; and walked over to Loddenden to have tea with Old Jane; and had a bonfire, the day Vin caught a bream, so that they could cook it in the embers, wrapped in wet paper.

For the last day they had made at least six different plans, but they were all out-of-door ones and it was obvious that they would all have to be abandoned. The sky was black and sagging, like an old tarpaulin. A big cross-channel plane was labouring unsteadily southward against the gale, flying so low that it looked as though it would barely clear the chimneys. Below the high wooded ridge on which their house stood the green and silver network of the Marsh lay blurred with rain, its dykes swollen and many of its pastures already merged in flood.

It had evidently got to be an indoor day. And because it was the last one they took turns, in order of age, at choosing what to do. Clem, who came first, chose darts; they played Round the Clock, and Nannie, as usual, won. Mrs. Miniver chose Letter Bags (a game which is to all other letter-games as dry-fly fishing is to a string and a bent pin). Nannie, most popularly, chose toffee-making on the nursery fire; and by the time that was set aside in biscuit-tin lids to cool, lunch was ready.

Afterwards they took another look at the weather. It was quite hopeless. The wind, no longer squally, had risen to a steady roar. The trees were straining, the lawn sodden, the Marsh completely blotted out. Vin chose charades, and Judy said she had been going to choose dressing up, so they combined the two; and that, of course, lasted them easily till tea-time.

Next it was Toby's turn. But all he wanted, apparently, and he wanted it with a consuming urgency, was to be left alone in a corner with eight elastic bands and an old photograph frame: he said he had had a good idea at tea. So the rest of them had a concert, with Clem at the piano. They sang 'Camptown Races' and 'The Ash Grove' and 'Rolling Down to Rio' and 'Alfonso Spagoni' and 'Cockles and Mussels' and 'A Bicycle Made for Two.' They were going to sing 'Home, Sweet Home,' but Vin suggested that it ought to be pronounced 'Hume, Sweet Hume,' like the surname; and after that, because they were just in the right mood for silly jokes, they laughed too much to be able to sing it at all, so the concert came to an end.

So far as they knew, Toby had been paying no attention. But when the noise of their own laughter had died away they became aware of a small reedy voice singing in the far corner, accompanied by a confused twangling sound. It was Toby, blissfully sweeping the strings of his good idea.

'"Carry me hume"' (he sang) '"to Old Virginny. . . ." Tck! That end band's come loose again.'

When the two younger ones had been taken off to bed, Vin went to the window and peered out at the dripping garden. The rain had stopped at last; a few torn clouds were racing past in a clear moonlit sky. But it was too late now. The holidays were over.

In Search of a Charwoman

ABOUT once a year Clem rather ruefully suggested, and
Mrs. Miniver reluctantly agreed, that it was about time
they asked the Lane-Pontifexes to dinner.

There was nothing really the matter with the Lane-
Pontifexes. They were quite nice, intelligent, decent people;
she was personable, and he was well-informed: yet for some
mysterious reason one's heart sank. Their company, as Clem
said, was a continual shutting of windows. They asked the
Minivers to dinner about every two months; it was impossible, without being churlish, to get out of it more than three
times running; and eventually, of course, they had to be asked
in return. This acquaintanceship had lasted, neither waxing
nor waning, for nearly ten years, and there seemed to be no
particular reason why it should ever come to an end. Clem
said it was part of the white man's burden.

Undiluted Lane-Pontifex was not to be thought of, so they
generally made it an excuse for asking as many people as their
dining-room table would hold, and that meant getting Mrs.
Jackman in to help with the washing-up. On the morning of
the dinner-party Mrs. Jackman sent a message to say that
she couldn't come after all, as her mother was queer. So
Mrs. Miniver, fervently wishing that the queerness of Mrs.
Jackman's mother had not happened to coincide with the immi-
nence of the Lane-Pontifexes, set off in search of a substitute.

She crossed the King's Road, turned up Skelton Street (which is not one of the streets that Chelsea shows to American visitors), and approached the towering red-brick jungle which is known as 'the Buildings.' Among the branches of this forest, theoretically at any rate, desirable and efficient charwomen hang in ripe clusters for the plucking; but the plucking is not so simple. The architectural style of the Buildings is Late Victorian Philanthropic. Each clump is named after a different benefactor, and each block in each clump is distinguished by a large capital letter. Mrs. Miniver entered the maze by the nearest gateway and then hesitated. She had heard of Mrs. Burchett through a friend, and she thought her address was No. 23 Platt's Dwellings; but she had reckoned without the alphabetical factor. She tried No. 23 in D Block, which happened to be near at hand, and after that she tried No. 23 in Blocks E, F, and G. But either the inhabitants genuinely did not know Mrs. Burchett's address, or else some esoteric code forbade them to reveal it. No. 23 was in every case on the fourth floor; and as she climbed up the steep stone stairs of Block H Mrs. Miniver felt inclined, quite unfairly, to blame the whole business on to the Lane-Pontifexes.

This time, however, she was more successful. A large, neat, cheerful woman came to the door, with her hair piled up on the top of her head like a whipped cream walnut. Obviously a pearl among charwomen – a capable pearl. Yes, she was Mrs. Burchett. Yes, she had often worked for Miss Ducane, and was glad that Miss Ducane had recommended her. Yes, she would certainly come along this evening and give a hand.

'To tell you the truth,' she added with gusto, 'I was just wishing summing like this would turn up. Not that I *need* to do cleaning at present, really, Burchett and the boys all being in work. In fact, my son Len, 'e says I've no business to go out to work at all, when there's others wanting it more. But there – I don't know whatever I should do if I didn't. Every now and then I just feel I've got to 'ave a bit of a fling.' She tossed the whipped cream walnut so that it quivered. 'Of course, charing. . . . I suppose it's on'y like clearing up somebody else's mess instead of your own, but it does make a change, and you do get a bit of company. Burchett, *'e* says, "You let 'er go, Len, and never mind the rights and wrongs. Coop 'er up too long, she gets *'ipped*. And goodness knows," 'e says, "when your mother gets 'ipped there's no peace for any of us till she's worked it off summow."'

She gave a large, good-humoured laugh. Mrs. Miniver liked her more and more, recognizing in her that most endearing of qualities, an abundant zest for life. It was rare, that zest, and it bore no relation to age, class, creed, moral worth, or intellectual ability. It was an accidental gift, like blue eyes or a double-jointed thumb: impossible to acquire, and almost impossible, thank heaven, to lose. To be completely without it was the worst lack of all – and it dawned on her in a flash that that was what was the matter with the Lane-Pontifexes.

'You'll come at seven, then?'

'I shan't be late,' said Mrs. Burchett, beaming reliably. It was evident that in spirit her sleeves were already rolled up.

Threading her way back between the serried barrows of Skelton Street, Mrs. Miniver asked herself which of them was right – Burchett or Len. Economically, Len, of course. But psychologically, Burchett: for pent-up volcanoes can do almost as much harm in the world as empty purses.

On the hall table there was a telephone message. Mr. and Mrs. Lane-Pontifex were extremely sorry, but they had both gone down with 'flu. Mrs. Miniver's heart gave a leap, and she immediately felt ashamed of herself. As an act of penitence she went out to the flower shop and sent the Lane-Pontifexes a big bunch of jonquils and a note. But nothing could undo the leap; and as she walked home for the second time, she reflected what possibilities the evening now held; how many lovely people there were from among whom they could fill the two empty places – people whom they really wanted to see, who were merry or wise or comforting or revealing, whose presence either heartened the spirit or kindled the mind; people who opened windows instead of shutting them. And she reflected, also, how many of the most enjoyable parties were achieved by taking away the number you first thought of.

The First Day of Spring

IT was a Wedgwood day, with white clouds delicately modelled in relief against a sky of pale pure blue. The best of England, thought Mrs. Miniver, as opposed to countries with reasonable climates, is that it is not only once a year that you can say, 'This is the first day of spring.' She had already said it twice since Christmas – once in January, when they had driven across the Marsh to the sea and it had been warm enough to lie on the sand without a coat; and once in February, when she had taken the children for a lunch picnic in Kensington Gardens. The grass had been scattered with twigs from the previous night's gale, and by the next afternoon it was snowing: but while it lasted that day had been part of the authentic currency of spring – a stray coin tossed down carelessly on account.

But this time, she thought (though she knew quite well that one said that every time), it really was spring. On her way downstairs she paused in the drawing-room to look at the plane branches which she had picked up on the Embankment when the men were lopping the trees. She did this every year, but she could never quite believe her eyes when they actually burst into bud. It seemed impossible that those neat emerald bobbles, those velvety, milky-green leaves, should have been implicit in the soot-black sticks – so much deader-looking than the polished brown twigs of the countryside – which she

had brought in a month ago. She bent closer to look at one of
the newest leaves (it was soft and half-spread, like a little
pointed paw), got a cloud of yellow pollen from the flowers
on to her nose, and went downstairs sneezing.

Outside the air was delicious. She could feel it stroking her
face as she moved through it, but there was no sensation of
either warmth or chill. Walking towards Westminster (she was
going to meet Clem for lunch near his office), she wondered
why she found this particular temperature so charming; and
decided that it was because, on a day like this, she came nearer
than usual to losing her sense of separate identity. Extremes of
heat and cold she enjoyed too, but it was with a tense, bel-
ligerent enjoyment. When they beat against the irregular
frontiers of the skin, with all its weak angles and vulnerable
salients, they made her acutely conscious of her own bound-
aries in space. Here, she would find herself thinking, is where
I end and the outside world begins. It was exciting, but divi-
sive: it made for loneliness. But on certain days, and this was
one of them, the barriers were down. She felt as though she
and the outside world could mingle and interpenetrate; as
though she was not entirely contained in her own body but
was part also of every other person in the street; and, for that
matter, of the thrush singing on a tree in Eaton Square, the
roan dray-horse straining to take up the load at Grosvenor
Place, the cat stepping delicately across Buckingham Palace
Road. This was the real meaning of peace – not mere absence
of division, but an active consciousness of unity, of being one
of the mountain-peak islands on a submerged continent.

Just beyond the entrance to the royal stables she became
aware that she was walking behind, and gradually overtaking,
a small, ragged boy. He was about Toby's size, but probably
older. His shorts, even though they had been hauled well up
under his armpits, were still far too long for him, and they
had a big cobbled patch on the seat; his grey jersey was dirty,
skimpy, and threadbare; his legs were spindly, his hair mouse-
coloured and closely cropped. He was not an attractive

urchin: but what caught her eye were his accoutrements. He wore a sword made out of two pieces of broken lath, hung round his middle with string; his helmet was a brown paper bag with a pigeon's feather stuck through it and 'Brooks's Stores' printed on it upside-down; and on his left arm he carried a home-made cardboard shield. His step was jaunty yet purposeful, as though he was setting off on some secret campaign in which he was confident of victory. (There were dragons in St. James's Park, she knew, for those who needed them: she had lived near it herself as a child.)

By the time he reached the front gates of the Palace she had drawn almost level with him: she could see that the shield was roughly coloured with red chalk and tied to his arm with a bootlace. She was about to pass him when he caught sight of another urchin, similarly equipped, on the opposite pavement. It was evidently going to be a combined expedition. He gave a shrill yell of greeting and stepped off the kerb.

'Look out!' cried Mrs. Miniver, grabbing him by the shoulder. A taxi swerved with screaming brakes and avoided him by perhaps an inch. But the boy was unimpressed.

'I'm awright,' he protested impatiently; shook himself free, and dashed out again into the road. Mrs. Miniver watched him till he got safely over to the other side. Then she discovered that her knees were trembling and that she felt extremely sick. Behind her the sentries stamped and strode, met, turned, and parted, carrying out with beautiful precision their antique ritual. Sentries and cardboard shields: parallel gestures, it seemed, in a world of bombing planes and motor traffic. But perhaps the making of the gesture was what mattered.

She pulled herself together and walked on. The water, a bright translucent curve, flowed steadily into the marble basin; the tritons, nereids, and dolphins gambolled along the frieze; the symbolic bronze statues held, a trifle sententiously, their heroic poses; and high above them all the gilt Queen sat calmly in the sun.

On Hampstead Heath

THEY went away nearly every week-end, either to Starlings or to other people's houses, but about once a month they made a point of staying in London. On Saturday afternoon they would drive down to see Vin at school, and on Sunday the two younger children would take it in turns to choose a treat. This time it was Toby's turn, and he chose Hampstead Heath because he wanted to sail his boat on the pond. Judy wasn't particularly keen on boats, but her favourite doll Christabel had a new spring coat and she was quite glad of a chance to take her out in it.

It was a clear, clean, nonchalant kind of day, with a billowy south wind. The scene round the pond, as they burst upon it suddenly up the hill, would have made an admirable opening for a ballet – a kind of English *Petrouchka* or *Beau Danube*. The blue pond, the white sails, the children in their Sunday clothes, the strolling grown-ups, the gambolling dogs, the ice-cream men (hatched out prematurely by the unseasonable heat) tinkling slowly round on their box-tricycles – it all had an air of having been rehearsed up to a perfection of spontaneity. The choreography was excellent, the décor charming: it remained to be seen whether any theme would develop.

When they got out of the car Toby discovered that he had left the key of his motor-boat at home. It was much too late to go back, of course: there was nothing to be done except wait

and see how he would take it. One never knew, when setting
out to comfort Toby, whether to prepare first aid for a pin-
prick or a broken heart. He was not yet old enough to be able
to grade his own misfortunes: it is one of the maturer accom-
plishments. Fortunately he was in a philosophical mood. He
just said: 'Oh, well, we can watch the others,' and trotted off
to the pond with Clem, his feet beating crotchets against his
father's minims.

Mrs. Miniver found a deck-chair and sat down in the sun.
Judy walked about, carrying Christabel rather ostentatiously
so that people could see her new coat. It was really magnificent – pale yellow tweed with a brown velvet collar and brown
buttons. Watching her, Mrs. Miniver wondered whether the
modern unbreakable dolls, which lasted for years, were more,
or less, precious to their owners than the old china ones, whose
expectation of life had been a matter of months. The old ones
had had the agonizing charm of transience: the modern ones
held the promise of a reliable and enduring companionship –
you could make plans for their future, think out their next
winter's wardrobe. But it was a silly problem, after all. For
love is no actuary: and a new-born baby was probably neither
more, nor less, treasured three hundred years ago than it is
now, in spite of all our statistics about infant mortality.

The sun was getting quite hot. From where she sat Mrs.
Miniver could see two street orators setting up their flimsy
platforms and angling for an audience. Judging by their
clothes and general demeanour she guessed that the one on the
right was Left-wing and the one on the left Right-wing: but
she was too far away to read the wording on their notice
boards, and when they began to speak nothing reached her
except a confused gabble, like a mix-up of stations on the
wireless. Seeing Clem and Toby leave the pond and walk over
towards the speakers, she collected Judy and joined them. As
soon as she got near she found that her guess had been wrong:
the right-hand speaker was extreme Right and the left extreme
Left. But how many of their audience, she wondered, would

have noticed if they had got up behind the wrong placards by mistake?

It was hard to take in the sense of what the speakers were saying, so confusing was the double clamour. But one thing was certain, that the fabric of both speeches was shot through and through with the steely tinsel of war. 'To combat the forces of tyranny . . .' one of them ranted. 'To crush down the menace of revolution . . .' mouthed the other just as glibly. 'Is any sacrifice too great . . .?' 'Which of us would not willingly lay down . . .?'

And now, from somewhere behind them, came the sound of a third voice, so shrill, reedy and raucous that it made itself heard even through the babel nearer at hand. It seemed only half human, and for a moment Mrs. Miniver had a sense of nightmare; but as soon as she realized what it was she grabbed Clem by the arm. 'Come on!' she said. 'There's a Punch and Judy!' Clem's face lit up. He hoisted Toby on to his shoulder and they all four edged their way out of the crowd.

The rest of the morning was pure bliss. For over an hour they stood, absorbed, while the immortal melodrama unfolded itself before their eyes. The proscenium was shabby, the properties crude, the puppets battered almost featureless by the years of savage slapstick they had undergone: but the performance was superb. The baby yelled and was flung out of the window; Judy scolded and was bludgeoned to death; the beadle, the doctor, and the hangman tried in turn to perform their professional duties and were outrageously thwarted; Punch, cunning, violent and unscrupulous, with no virtues whatever except humour and vitality, came out triumphant in the end. And all the children, their faces upturned in the sun like a bed of pink daisies, laughed and clapped and shouted with delight.

'So what?' said Mrs. Miniver at the end, to Clem.

'So nothing,' said Clem, shrugging his shoulders. 'It's great art, that's all. Come on, I'm hungry.'

A Country House Visit

THEY went to Cornwall for Easter, to stay with the Edward Havelocks.

People who didn't know Mrs. Miniver very well, and even some of those who did, would have found it difficult to believe what a feeling of leaden oppression always came over her during the last few miles of the approach to a strange country house visit. If they were arriving in their own car she could comment on it half-jokingly to Clem, which helped to dispel it: but if, as now, they had come by train and been met at the station, she could only watch the back of the chauffeur's neck in dumb dismay, or at the most make some cryptic reference to her state of mind.

'These modern tumbrils are so *fast*,' she said in an agonized murmur to Clem as the car swept them all too rapidly towards Penzarron.

'Look!' said Clem. 'More standing stones. This place must have been stiff with Druids.' He was not unfeeling, but he thought, quite rightly, that she ought to have grown out of this by now. Also he knew that her panic would disappear the moment she set foot in the house, and that she would most likely end by enjoying herself. Mrs. Miniver knew all this, too, in her mind, but she could never quite succeed in transferring the knowledge to the pit of her stomach.

It wasn't shyness: she had never experienced that. She got on easily with strangers, and there were few things she enjoyed more than that first tentative groping among wavelengths, followed – if you were unlucky – by a Talk on Accountancy, but far more often, thank heaven, by a burst of music. No, it wasn't shyness. It was more like a form of claustrophobia – a dread of exchanging the freedom of her own self-imposed routine for the inescapable burden of somebody else's. She must be prepared to adjust herself all day to an alien tempo: to go out, to come in, to go to bed, to sit, to stride, to potter (oh! worst of all, to potter), whenever her hostess gave the hint. There was always a chance, of course, that the Havelocks' tempo might turn out to be the same as her own: that they might hate sitting long over meals; walk quickly or not at all; enjoy arguments, jokes, and silences, but detest making conversation; and realize that a day without a chunk or two of solitude in it is like a cocktail without ice.

There was certainly a chance: but at moments like this it seemed a very remote one. They had come out on to the coast road now, and Cornwall was out-postering itself, as usual, with rocky headlands and sandy coves and fishing villages that spilled themselves down the cliff face like cascades of mesembryanthemum. The year was older here: the oakwoods were rounded, cushiony and mustard-gold, the grass under the fruit trees was already scattered with petals, the cottage gardens were little glowing squares of rich embroidery. It was being a lavishly lovely spring, almost frightening in its perfection, as though for some reason it was meant to be a final performance. 'Positively the last appearance on any stage. . . .' She suggested this to Clem, wondering whether by any chance it had struck him, too.

'But that's what I feel every spring,' said Clem unexpectedly. And I've known him through seventeen of them, thought Mrs. Miniver, without knowing that. But it was quite natural really: she had long ago discovered that whereas words, for her, clarified feelings, for Clem, on the whole, they obscured them. This was perhaps just as well. For if they had both been equally explicit they might have been in danger of understanding each other completely; and a certain degree of un-understanding (not mis-, but un-) is the only possible sanctuary which one human being can offer to another in the midst of the devastating intimacy of a happy marriage.

She saw every relationship as a pair of intersecting circles. The more they intersected, it would seem at first glance, the better the relationship; but this is not so. Beyond a certain point the law of diminishing returns sets in, and there aren't enough private resources left on either side to enrich the life that is shared. Probably perfection is reached when the area of the two outer crescents, added together, is exactly equal to that of the leaf-shaped piece in the middle. On paper there must be some neat mathematical formula for arriving at this: in life, none. She breathed surreptitiously on the window of the car and drew two circles with her finger; but they hardly intersected at all – a mere moonlight infatuation which would soon peter out – so she added ears and whiskers and turned them into Siamese-twin cats. (But would that count, she wondered, as being Siamese cats?) Then she met the chauffeur's eye in the driving-mirror and hurriedly rubbed the whole thing out, pretending to peer at the view.

'But it's all right,' said Clem, pursuing his own train of thought. 'She always decides to stage another come-back.'

'Who? Oh – spring. Yes.' But she could not respond with much gaiety, for they were actually turning in at the gates of Penzarron. This was the worst moment of all. There was no escape now. In four days' time, she told herself, they would be on their way back to London, having probably made several new friends: but somehow this was no comfort to her at all. At any rate, she thought, clinging to a straw, she had just bought herself a really grand dressing-gown, the kind one always caught glimpses of, exquisitely laid out, through other women's bedroom doors. The vision of it sustained her all the way up the drive between the mountainous rhododendron combers which never quite broke on top of the car.

And all of a sudden the ordeal was over, and they had arrived, and Leila Havelock was introducing them to their fellow-guests; and the tuning-knobs were turning, turning, in broad preliminary arcs, ready for more delicate adjustment as soon as the first faint throbbing of music should beat upon the ear.

Mrs. Downce

T HE first week-end after the school holidays were over, the Minivers kept away from Starlings, so as to let Mrs. Downce give the house a thorough turning out. By the time they went down again it was well into May. A noticeable change had come over the countryside: it had lost the coltish uncertain grace of spring and taken on a more poised, though still virginal, loveliness.

As soon as Mrs. Downce appeared at the door Mrs. Miniver knew, with that morbid sensitiveness to emotional atmosphere which is common to lovers and housewives, that something was amiss. She was not sure which of the two possible types of bad weather the omens portended – the subjective (or dudgeonly) or the objective (or catastrophic). On the whole, knowing that it couldn't be anything to do with the children, she hoped that it would turn out to be the latter. Burst water-mains were so much easier to deal with than injured feelings. But mightn't it, after all, be something to do with the children? There might have been a telephone message while they were on their way down—

'Is everything all right?' she asked in a casual voice, pulling off her gloves.

'Well, no, madam, I'm afraid I couldn't hardly say that.' Mrs. Downce paused ominously.

'*(Oh, come on, you old fool, don't keep me on tenterhooks like this – which of them is it? Toby? Judy? Vin?)* I'm sorry to hear that. What's happened?'

'Well, madam, there's nothing what you could call happened, it's just there's a norrible smell.'

Mrs. Miniver nearly laughed out loud with relief.

'Smell? Where?'

'Everywhere, madam. All over the back part of the house, that is. A *norrible* smell.'

Mrs. Miniver crossed the hall, opened the door which led to the kitchen premises, and shut it again very quickly.

'Good heavens!' she said. 'It's unspeakable.'

Mrs. Downce's face bore the triumphant look peculiar to those who, suspected of hyperbole, are found to have been employing meiosis.

'Downce thinks it's the drains. His mother died of typhoid.'

Clem came in from putting away the car.

'Look here, Clem, *you* ought to know – is this drains, or isn't it?'

'I'm an architect,' said Clem, 'not a sanitary inspector. Still, I'll have a sniff – oh, Lord!' He, too, shut the passage door, appalled.

'Me and Downce have been sitting in the library, sir, and cooking on a spirit lamp. We thought you wouldn't mind.'

'Of course not,' said Clem. 'But why on earth didn't you get in a plumber?'

'We thought at first it might go off,' Mrs. Downce explained. 'But when it got too bad we did ring up Mr. Bateman. But that's three days ago now – he's putting in a new bathroom up at the Hall, and you know what the tradesmen are like down here when they're busy. Independent. *They* don't care *who* gets typhoid.' She was a Cockney, but had married into Kent; and the last twenty-five years had only strengthened her conviction that anywhere outside London was virtually Central Africa.

'Nobody's going to get typhoid,' said Clem impatiently, striding over to the telephone.

'It's Saturday afternoon, sir,' Mrs. Downce reminded him with melancholy relish. 'You won't get nobody now till Monday.'

'Come on,' said Mrs. Miniver, in whom curiosity had at last overcome squeamishness. 'Let's try and find out what it is. It may not be drains at all. It may be a dead rat under the floor.'

'Bore like a dead sheep,' said Clem, as, holding their noses, they proceeded down the kitchen passage.

'Bore like a dead babboth,' said Mrs. Miniver. They tracked the smell past the kitchen, scullery, and larder, until they came to the small wash-place and cloakroom just inside the garden door, where it seemed to be at its worst.

'I suppose that beads it bust be draids,' said Mrs. Miniver. But Clem, after looking round suspiciously among the litter of waterproofs, walking-sticks, nets, rods, and golf-clubs, took down Vin's fishing haversack from a hook on the wall.

'Bait,' he said briefly. '*Dab* the boy.' They carried the haversack out into the garden and emptied it. Among the floats, leads, and other paraphernalia there were two tins. The first contained earthworms, the second lugworms, both in an indescribable state.

'Really,' said Mrs. Miniver, 'this is a bit much. Such waste, too,' she added. 'I helped him dig those lugworms the day we went over to Dungeness. They took us nearly two hours to get.'

Clem's face was grim. He got a spade from the tool-shed and buried the bait very deep in the kitchen garden. Then he went indoors and wrote a letter to Vin. From the time it took, and the look of his shoulder-blades, Mrs. Miniver was afraid that for once in a way he was being over-stern; but when he leant back in his chair to re-read the letter she saw that it was profusely illustrated down the margin with his own particular brand of pin-man picture: so she knew it was all right. And Mrs. Downce, as she brought in the tea, remarked amiably and with an air of discovery that boys would be boys. Mrs. Miniver breathed more freely. The trough of low pressure was already over: it was going to be a fine week-end.

Married Couples

'WE might get the Danbys,' said Mrs. Miniver, looking through her address-book over early morning tea. Clem's father had just sent them a salmon, and it seemed a good opportunity to ask a few people to dinner.

'We-ell,' said Clem, 'I'd love to have Nigel, but I don't feel like coping with Helen. She yatters.'

'What about the Pritchards?'

'There again,' said Clem. 'Only the other way round. It would be grand to see Sara again, but Clive'll talk nothing but shop. It's too hot for Clive. Look – I must go and shave. Call out if you get any other ideas.'

Mrs. Miniver put down the address-book and poured out some more tea. As she did so her eye fell on an article in the newspaper which Clem had just thrown aside. 'Problems of Marriage,' ran the title. She glanced through the first paragraph.

'I am not setting out to decry marriage. Nobody pretends that it is a perfect institution, but nobody has yet suggested a better one. At the worst it is seldom quite beyond repair: at the best it can be delightful. Most married people are neither more nor less happy than they would have been if they had remained single. They may not be able to go round the world on a tramp steamer: but there is not that start in the evening when the coal falls out of the grate.'

Good of its kind, she thought; written, at any rate, with more restraint and a lighter touch than most articles on that well-worn subject: though, like all the rest of them, it bristled with three-quarter truths. She would finish reading it later, when she had settled the dinner question.

She applied herself again to the address-book. The Frants? The Palmers? Really, it was lamentable, the unevenness of most married couples. Like those gramophone records with a superb tune on one side and a negligible fill-up on the other which you had to take whether you wanted it or not. Only in this case you could not simply ignore the vapid backing, but were forced to play it through to the bitter end exactly the same number of times as the side which you treasured. How silly it was, this convention – relaxed a little nowadays but still surprisingly obstinate – that you must not invite one half of a married couple to dinner without the other. Even when both were equally charming, she often wished she could ask them on different days. For in order that the game of dinner-table conversation may be played to its best advantage, it is essential that every player should have a free hand. He must be at liberty to assume disguises, to balance precariously in untenable positions, to sacrifice the letter of the truth to the spirit of it. And somehow the partner's presence makes this difficult. She does not, if she is civilized, chip in with 'No, darling, it was Tuesday'; but she is apt to crumble the bread, and to have a look in her eye. The pronouns, of course, can be reversed, thought Mrs. Miniver hastily, remembering Clive and Sara.

'Any luck?' said Clem, reappearing.

'No, none whatever. All the couples we owe dinners to are hopelessly lopsided.'

'I wish to goodness,' said Clem, 'we were as brave as old Lady J. She simply asks all the nice halves to one party and all the boaks to another.'

'I know. And as often as not she has a cold and cancels the boak party at the last minute. But anyway, old Lady J.'s a

Character. You can't do that sort of thing unless you're a Character.'

'Oh, well, better ask both lots, and then you can talk to Nigel, and I can talk to Sara, and Helen and Clive can go into a boakish huddle.'

'All right,' said Mrs. Miniver, shutting up the address-book with relief. But why, oh why, she wondered, do writers of articles on marriage always confine themselves to the difficulties which it presents to those who are actually involved in it, and never mention the problems which it raises for their friends? To everybody except the protagonists, she thought for the thousandth time, marriage is nothing but a nuisance. A single person is a manageable entity, whom you can either make friends with or leave alone. But half of a married couple is not exactly a whole human being: if the marriage is successful it is something a little more than that; if unsuccessful, a little less. In either case, a fresh complication is added to the already intricate business of friendship: as Clem had once remarked, you might as well try to dance a tarantella with a Siamese twin.

That had been years ago, before they were married; but the phrase had stuck, and to avoid, so far as their friendships were concerned, turning into Siamese twins had been one of their private marriage vows. How well, she wondered, had they kept it? Only their friends could judge: but even to have been aware of the danger was something.

A Drive to Scotland

Although they had driven up to Scotland every summer for fifteen years, they still felt a little stab of excitement when they came to the signpost at the top of Finchley Road which pointed to the left and simply said 'The North.' It made a kind of chapter-heading to their holiday.

They always started at seven after an early breakfast and shared the driving between them, changing over every fifty miles or so. This year it had been Clem's turn to take the wheel first, of which Mrs. Miniver was rather glad. It meant that during the dreary flat expanse between Biggleswade and Stamford she would be pleasantly preoccupied with driving, whereas she would be free, as passenger, to look about her at the beauty of the next stretch, which lay along the eastern fringe of the Dukeries. It was an ample, rolling, opulent beauty; Georgian, somehow, with a suggestion of full-bottomed wigs and old port. A trifle oppressive to live with, perhaps: but, as a rich dark-green tapestry drawn smoothly and swiftly past one, very satisfying. At Retford they changed places again. This landed Mrs. Miniver with Doncaster, the only big town on the whole route; but after that she had an easy drive across the Plain of York to Boroughbridge, where they stopped for lunch. The great point was that Clem now came in for Leeming Lane, a fast fifteen-mile stretch, as straight as an arrow, which he loved and could do justice to:

while she herself could sit back, enjoying the speed but
thankful that she wasn't at the wheel.

At Scotch Corner they swung off to the left towards
Bowes; and this, they always felt, was where 'The North'
really began, spiritually if not geographically. For they were
out of the plain at last and climbing up into a completely different country, a country of small steep tumbled fields, rough
stone walls, crying sheep, skirling plover, and lonely farm-
houses sheltered by clumps of sycamore.

'This,' said Clem as they topped a rise, 'is where we passed
those gipsies two years ago.'

'I know,' said Mrs. Miniver. 'I was just thinking that. With
the skewbald horse.' It was amazing, the number of little
memory-flags with which, on their minds' map, the road was
studded. There were dozens of them now, and every year
added a few more. There was one, for instance, near
Colsterworth, where their first car (a two-cylinder roller-skate
with overhead valves and partially exposed viscera, very sweet
and willing but extremely second-hand) had dropped a push-
rod; which, after a long search, they had recovered from the
gutter a quarter of a mile behind. And there was another flag
at the point where their third car (a meretricious black beast
of an obscure continental make, the only really disloyal one
they had ever owned) had venomously run a big end, strand-
ing them for fourteen hours at a tin garage by the roadside. It
had rained nearly the whole day; they had played countless
games of piquet on the top of a packing-case, and Clem had
scored repique and capot twice running. There were flags,
too, at all the places where they had ever stopped to picnic;
and one at the place where they had seen a particularly fine
double rainbow; and one at the place where, after rounding a
sharp bend, they had come upon a man in a stationary car
hurriedly removing his false black beard. An enigmatic flag,
that, five years old. They had, of course, lurked in the next
side-turning to let him pass, and then trailed him for miles;
but he took the Rotherham fork at Barnby Moor, so they

never discovered whether what they had seen was the after-
math of a practical joke or part of a real-life Buchan.

They were climbing steadily now; and presently the bones
of the earth began breaking through the grass in rocky scars
and outcrops; and higher still there were no fields at all, but
only bare moors. At the summit of the road, half-way
between Bowes and Brough, they stopped, according to their
invariable custom, and got out to stretch, smoke, and enjoy
the view. They were standing on the spine of England, nearly
fifteen hundred feet above the sea. Yorkshire lay behind,
Westmorland in front; Hunderthwaite Moor and Teesdale to
the north of them, Stainmore Forest and Arkengarthdale to
the south. The silence, after the monotonous hum of the car,
was almost startling. The air was knife-keen and as fresh as
lettuce. It seemed a far cry from the lush, matronly, full-
blown landscape of the south through which they had set out
that morning. Moving northward in space, thought Mrs.
Miniver, they had moved backward in time; reversed the irre-
versible, recaptured in late summer the feeling of spring. By
what analogous mental journey, she wondered, what deliber-
ate pilgrimage of the heart, could one – but she did not
pursue that metaphor: it would give her the slip, she felt, like
the man with the false beard.

Clem finished his cigarette and ground it out carefully with
his heel: the grass was tinder-dry. They got into the car again,
conscious that one of their most cherished flags was now
stuck in more deeply than ever. Mrs. Miniver let the clutch in
and set off on the long descent to Appleby. In the convex
driving-mirror she could see, dwindling rapidly, the patch of
road where they had stood; and she wondered why it had
never occurred to her before that you cannot successfully navigate the future unless you keep always framed beside it a
small, clear image of the past.

The Twelfth of August

'WELL,' said Archie McQuern, knocking out his pipe on the lowest stone of the dyke and brushing a crumb of pastry off his kilt. 'I suppose we'd better be moving on.'

He hoisted himself out of the heather and blew his whistle. Bess, the young black pointer, leapt to her feet; Duke and Reiver, the two liver-and-white ones, got to theirs more circumspectly, as befitted their age and experience. They all three stood looking up at him with their queer angular faces. It just shows, thought Mrs. Miniver, leaning back against the dyke and watching her brother-in-law, how careful one ought to be about what animals one gets mixed up with. Archie, tall, bony, and chestnut-headed, had been breeding pointers for twenty years and was now almost indistinguishable from Duke; while Alison, his eldest daughter, who was black-haired and who helped him to train them, was beginning to have a distinct look of Bess, especially about the eyes. Oh, well, there were worse things to look like: at any rate pointers had interesting faces, more intellectual and less sentimental than those of other gun-dogs. And she wondered, in passing, whether the narrow jaws and protruding teeth which are so distressingly prevalent among the English might not be due less to heredity than to their being encouraged to keep rabbits in their impressionable youth. Change a nation's pets and you might change its physiognomy: but she could not think, off-hand, of a nice prognathous substitute.

'No, thank you,' she said, in answer to a question from her brother-in-law. 'I don't think I'll walk the Laosgainn beats — I'll stay here with Susan and join you again when you're doing the Low Moor.'

The morning had been enjoyable but strenuous. Archie never dreamed of driving until he had had at least a fortnight of the subtler sport of shooting over dogs, so that the Twelfth at Quern, for onlookers, was not a ladylike affair of lolling in a grouse-butt with a well-powdered nose. It entailed a long and stiffish walk, some of it through very deep old heather. Mrs. Miniver loved it, especially now that she had Vin's shooting to watch as well as Clem's; but she was always glad enough to drop out while they did the two steepest beats of all, above the hill loch.

The guns trudged off up the lee side of the dyke. The van, loaded with empty luncheon-baskets and the morning's bag, blundered away down the cart-track like a drunken bee. The two women moved over to a little grassy knoll shaded by rowan trees. The wind had dropped entirely; it was as hot as one always forgets the Highlands can be. Ben Cailleach and the other high tops were shimmering. Below, they could see the grey roof of Quern House jutting out of its fir plantation, with a column of smoke going up from the kitchen chimney as straight as a wand. Beyond lay the little strath dotted with haycocks, and beyond that again Judy and Toby and their two youngest cousins were busily damming the burn. It was good for them, thought Mrs. Miniver, to be for a time part of a large family, with the greater complexity, but lower intensity, of its relationships.

She brought her eyes back again from the hazy middle distance to the near, clear presence of Clem's sister, who had planted her back firmly against one of the rowans and begun to knit.

'Susan,' said Mrs. Miniver, 'where did that knitting come

from? I swear you didn't have any on you a minute ago. I believe you materialize bits of knitting out of thin air, the way conjurers do with lighted cigarettes.'

'No,' said Susan, 'they grow out of my finger-tips, like a thread out of a spider. As a matter of fact my whole inside is made of wool. One gets like that, you know, living in the Highlands all the year round.'

'The great thing about you,' said her sister-in-law, 'is that you've never let it spread from the neck up.'

'Oh, well,' said Mrs. McQuern elliptically, 'there's always Douglas and Foulis.'

Mrs. Miniver lay down on her side to make the colours of the hills clearer. Across the foreground of her picture was a spray of whin in full bloom, upon which two chaffinches were swinging. Above them a pair of white butterflies were weaving quick flirtatious patterns in the air. It was idyllic – a Chinese painting on silk; an exquisite, peaceful oasis in a day of organized death.

'It's all very well to talk like that,' she said. 'But you know you wouldn't live anywhere else for the world. I believe you're completely and utterly contented.'

Susan chuckled. 'Not always. Not when the cook breaks her leg on the eleventh of August.'

'Oh, everybody has catastrophes. The only thing that matters is to be properly cast, so that you get the kind of catastrophes you can deal with. I think that's what I meant, more than contented. You're quite perfectly cast, Susan.'

'Bah-hah,' said Susan. 'So are you, for that matter. I'd hate your sort of life just as much as you'd hate mine.'

'Except for a holiday – yes.'

'In fact,' said Susan, 'it's just as important to marry the right life as the right person.'

Well, no, thought Mrs. Miniver, not quite. But near enough for a hot day, after lunch. She shut her eyes, taking the Chinese picture with her inside the lids.

'Listen!' said Susan, presently. 'I heard a shot.'

Mrs. Miniver opened her eyes again for a moment. Eight white wings lay scattered on the grass under the gorsebush. The chaffinches were looking as though butterflies wouldn't melt in their mouths. It was too hot to work out the moral. She shut her eyes again and went to sleep.

At the Games

THEY all went over to the Crurie Games, though not all for the same reason. Archie McQuern went because he thought he ought to, and Susan went because Archie thought she ought to. The three Miniver children and the four younger McQuerns went because of the Fun Fair in the next field. Alison, the eldest, went because the Ardbennie party were sure to be there, and she knew that Jock Murray was home on leave. Miss Bates, the English holiday governess, who had never been in Scotland before, went because her great-grandmother's name had been Gillespie, and the sound of pipe-music always made her feel pleasantly queer. Clem went because he would generally rather do things than not, and Mrs. Miniver went because for some obscure reason she liked watching Highland Games.

'I can't understand it,' said her sister-in-law. 'I shouldn't have thought it was your line at all. Just look how you go on about cricket.'

But the whole point was, Mrs. Miniver tried to explain, that the Games weren't cricket. In fact, they weren't games at all, but athletics. There was no team spirit about, and no holiness and winning of Waterloo, but only a lot of ordinary men, each one out for himself, trying to run faster or vault higher or throw a weight farther than any of the others for the sake of thirty or forty shillings in prize-money and a mention in the *Crurie Herald*. It might not be very heroic, but it was agreeably straightforward.

And beautiful, too, she thought with a lift of pleasure as one of the vaulters soared smoothly upwards at the end of his banded pole, cleared an improbable height, and dropped to the ground as lightly as though he were falling through water. (For some reason, pole-vaulting always gave the impression that it was being performed in slow-motion.) He was a lean, lantern-jawed man in a darned sweater and faded blue shorts. He straightened himself up, strolled back to the starting-point, and pulled on his trousers. The next-but-one competitor was just taking his off. They were all completely unconcerned. Miss Bates looked as though she wasn't quite sure of her ground.

'It must be dreadfully cold for them, poor things,' she said at last, taking the broader view.

It certainly was cold for the middle of August. The occasional gleams of sun were as unconvincing as a forced smile, and most of the time a bitter little wind enfiladed the grandstand, sending coat-collars up and hands into pockets. There was a burst of applause. An announcement boomed out from the four loud-speakers which clustered back to back like the florets of moschatel. Mrs. Miniver turned to her brother-in-law.

'What was that? I missed it.'

'Heavy hammer,' said Archie. 'Willie Muir is going to try and break the ground record. He's the local blacksmith.'

Mrs. Miniver touched Miss Bates on the arm and pointed to the farther side of the field. Muir was a huge man. His chest muscles stood out through his thin singlet and his kilt was the size of a barrel. He stepped forward, rubbed his hands, stamped his toes into the ground to get a firm stance, and gripped the haft of the hammer.

'Good gracious!' said Miss Bates, appalled, as he began to whirl the hammer round his head and shoulders, slowly at first but with increasing speed. 'Look, there are some people sitting quite close to him – supposing he let go at the wrong moment?'

Mrs. Miniver had often supposed this, with horrified fascination; but it never seemed to happen. The hammer was whirling now at a great speed, and at last Muir swung right round with a kind of grunting groan, and twenty-two pounds of brute metal flew through the air, landing with a thump a few feet from the judges. Mrs. Miniver relaxed. There was a storm of applause. Two men measured the distance with a tape. It was announced as ninety-four feet – three inches longer than the ground record. The applause redoubled.

'Well,' said Miss Bates, 'I suppose that's what they call tossing the caber. Or is it cabber?'

'Caber,' said Mrs. Miniver. 'No, that wasn't it, but you'll see it in a minute, I expect.'

Meanwhile several other things were going on in the picture which was framed by the heather-trimmed pillars of the grand-stand (stuck here and there, incongruously enough, with dahlias). The competitors were just assembling for the 600 yards handicap, looking, as runners so often do before a race, like the criminal line-up in a gangster film – to be transformed by the starter's pistol into Greek gods. In another corner of the field a pair of wrestlers were interlocked in one of the more intimate holds of the catch-as-catch-can style. Miss Bates looked away rather quickly. The quadruple loudspeaker was announcing that the lantern-jawed man had won the pole-vaulting with a height of ten feet nine inches. In the far distance the steam organ of the roundabout was playing, sweetly and puffily, 'My Lily of Laguna.' And on the wooden platform in front of the grand-stand two men in full Highland dress were poised for a sword-dance. One of them was small and spare, with light eyes, like Alan Breck. He wore the striking black-and-yellow of the MacLeods; there was a sprig of juniper in his bonnet. The second was younger and taller. He was wearing a dark greenish tartan, and his lips were parted all the time in an almost imperceptible smile.

The pipes struck up their sharp thrusting rhythm, drowning the faint noises of the fair-ground. The two men danced neatly and vigorously, with a passionate precision. Their pointed soft-shod feet twinkled unerringly between the crossed blades and scabbards, in and out and over and round, going through the old intricate ritual with which their forebears had woven themselves a cloak of security on the eve of battle. But now, if toe touched steel, it would mean only the forfeiting of prize-money, not a chill in the heart at the certainty of impending death.

The younger man, as nimble as a cat for all his height, was still smiling a little as he danced. The Alan Breck one was flashing like a wasp in his black-and-yellow. The music began to quicken intolerably for the final steps: and Mrs. Miniver saw the rest of it through a mist. For I defy anyone, she thought in self-defence, to watch a sword-dance through to the end without developing a great-grandmother called Gillespie.

The Autumn Flit

'WHERE on earth is Vin?' asked Mrs. Miniver. The car was standing at the door of Starlings, ready to take them all back to London. The luggage-boot was filled to overflowing with the well-known paraphernalia of a nursery flit: even Clem's genius for stacking had been unable to make it look like anything but a cubist cornucopia. Clem was in the driving seat; Nannie was at the back, with Toby on her knee and Judy sitting close up beside her to make room for Vin. But Vin himself was nowhere to be seen.

'Wretched boy,' said Clem amiably. 'I told him what time we were starting.'

'He went off on his bike directly after breakfast,' said Judy, 'to fetch his knife. He left it over at Pound Mill yesterday when he was fishing.'

'He may have come in through the garden door,' said his mother. 'Mrs. Downce, you might go and see if he's in the kitchen, and I'll try the nursery.'

She went back into the house. It had already begun to acquire that out-at-grass, off-duty look which houses get as soon as their owners go away; it was quite obviously preparing to take off its stays and slip into something loose.

The day nursery was empty, but around it, like a line of salt wrack, lay unmistakable traces of the children. As they grew older the flotsam of the holidays, without diminishing

in quantity, changed a little in character. There were fewer
stones and pieces of wood, though Toby still collected flints
with holes through them and sticks which had been spirally
grooved by honeysuckle. On the other hand there were now
things like empty cartridge-cases (spent by Vin on rabbits
and retrieved by Toby for use in a vast chess-like game which
he played, by himself, on the squares of the nursery
linoleum); and on the edge of the window-sill lay some bright
shreds of wool, silk, and tinsel, some broken feathers, and the
clamp-marks of a small vice. Vin, the evening before, had
been tying flies; having run out of proper materials, he had
had to fall back on the contents of the toy-cupboard, and
with great ingenuity he had produced something which
looked at first sight like an Alexandra, but which was really,
he admitted, a Red-Indian-and-Gollywog.

Of Judy the traces were less conspicuous: her activities
were mostly personal and required little gear. But just occasionally she too was bitten with the boys' mania for making
things, and when that happened she got it badly. A few days
ago, someone had described in the 'Children's Hour' how to
make a reed-pipe out of a jointed wheat-stalk, or, failing that,
out of a drinking straw with a blob of sealing wax at one end.
The farms immediately round Starlings were all pasture and
hops: so she begged a packet of straws from Mrs. Downce
and used up every one of them. To make the vibrating tongue
was fairly easy, but to space the six finger-holes so as to get a
sol-fa scale proved to be a matter of trial and error, exasperating to herself and excruciating to her hearers. She cut her
left hand and burnt her right one. The floor became littered
with small square chips of straw: there was one now, lurking
under the table. Every half-hour or so there would be heard a
tentative tweedling cadence, full of quarter-tones and other
exotic intervals; then a sigh as she snipped off the unsuccessful part of the pipe and threw it away. (The top half she
thoughtfully preserved as a squeaker for Toby.) Just before
bed-time the next day she managed to produce a pipe on

which, by overblowing a little on the *la*, she could give a recognizable rendering of 'Drink to Me Only.'

As it happened, that day had been for the grown-ups one of great tension and anxiety, with the threat of war hanging like a leaden nimbus in the air. And Mrs. Miniver had drawn a curious comfort from watching Judy's small intent face, bent hour after hour over her delicate and absorbing task. International tempers might flame or cool; the turning kaleidoscope of time might throw mankind's little coloured scraps of belief into new patterns, new ideologies; but the length of the vibrating column of air which, in a tube of a given calibre, would produce C natural – that was one of the fixed things. And it wasn't the fault of the scientists, was it, if the people for whom they made the pipes chose to play dangerous tunes?

She went back to the car, and at the same moment Vin appeared from the direction of the bicycle-shed, very much out of breath.

'Sorry,' he said shortly, and scrambled into place beside Judy. Mrs. Miniver got in too. The car moved off through winding lanes towards the arterial road. It was certainly a heart-breaking day on which to leave the country. It was warm and yet fresh; blindfold, one could have mistaken it for a morning in early May: but this kind of day, she reflected, had a more poignant loveliness in autumn than in spring, because it was a receding footfall, a waning moon. The woods were just beginning to turn, the different trees springing into individuality again, demobilized from the uniform green of summer. There had been a heavy dew. From the row of fires in front of the hop-pickers' huts the smoke rose blue and pungent. The hops were nearly all in, the stripped bines lay tumbled and tangled on the ground. One campaign at least was over without bloodshed.

Gas Masks

CLEM had to go and get his gas mask early, on his way to the office, but the rest of them went at half-past one, hoping that the lunch hour would be less crowded. It may have been: but even so there was a longish queue. They were quite a large party – Mrs. Miniver and Nannie; Judy and Toby; Mrs. Adie, the Scots cook, lean as a winter aspen, and Gladys, the new house-parlourmaid: a pretty girl, with complicated hair. Six of them – or seven if you counted Toby's Teddy bear, which seldom left his side, and certainly not if there were any treats about. For to children, even more than to grown-ups (and this is at once a consolation and a danger), any excitement really counts as a treat, even if it is a painful excitement like breaking your arm, or a horrible excitement like seeing a car smash, or a terrifying excitement like playing hide-and-seek in the shrubbery at dusk. Mrs. Miniver herself had been nearly grown-up in August 1914, but she remembered vividly how her younger sister had exclaimed with shining eyes, 'I say! I'm in a war!'

But she clung to the belief that this time, at any rate, children of Vin's and Judy's age had been told beforehand what it was all about, had heard both sides, and had discussed it themselves with a touching and astonishing maturity. If the worst came to the worst (it was funny how one still shied away from saying, 'If there's a war,' and fell back on euphemisms) – if the worst came to the worst, these children would at least know that we were fighting against an idea, and not against a nation. Whereas the last generation had been told to run and play in the garden, had been shut out from the grown-ups' worried conclaves: and then quite suddenly had all been plunged into an orgy of licensed lunacy, of boy-cotting Grimm and Struwwelpeter, of looking askance at their cousins' old Fräulein, and of feeling towards Dachshund puppies the uneasy tenderness of a devout churchwoman dandling her daughter's love-child. But this time those lunacies – or rather, the outlook which bred them – must not be allowed to come into being. To guard against that was the most important of all the forms of war work which she and other women would have to do: there are no tangible gas masks to defend us in war-time against its slow, yellow, drifting corruption of the mind.

The queue wormed itself on a little. They moved out of the bright, noisy street into the sunless corridors of the Town Hall. But at least there were benches to sit on. Judy produced pencils and paper (she was a far-sighted child) and began playing Consequences with Toby. By the time they edged up to the end of the corridor Mr. Chamberlain had met Shirley Temple in a Tube lift and Herr Hitler was closeted with Minnie Mouse in an even smaller rendezvous.

When they got into the Town Hall itself they stopped playing. Less than half an hour later they came out again into the sunlit street: but Mrs. Miniver felt afterwards that during that half-hour she had said good-bye to something. To the last shreds which lingered in her, perhaps, of the old, false, traditional conception of glory. She carried away with her, as well as a litter of black rubber pigs, a series of detached impressions, like shots in a quick-cut film. Her own right hand with a pen in it, filling up six yellow cards in pleasura-ble block capitals; Mrs. Adie sitting up as straight as a ramrod under the fitter's hands, betraying no signs of the apprehen-sion which Mrs. Miniver knew she must be feeling about her

false fringe; Gladys's rueful giggle as her elaborate coiffure
came out partially wrecked from the ordeal; the look of
sudden realization in Judy's eyes just before her face was covered up; the back of Toby's neck, the valley deeper than usual
because his muscles were taut with distaste (he had a horror of
rubber in any form); a very small child bursting into a wail of
dismay on catching sight of its mother disguised in a black
snout; the mother's muffled reassurances – 'It's on'y Mum,
duck. Look – it's just a mask, like at Guy Fawkes, see?' (*Mea
mater mala sus est.* Absurdly, she remembered the Latin catch
Vin had told her, which can mean either 'My mother is a bad
pig' or 'Run, mother, the pig is eating the apples.')

Finally, in another room, there were the masks themselves,
stacked close, covering the floor like a growth of black fungus.
They took what had been ordered for them – four medium
size, two small – and filed out into the street.

It was for this, thought Mrs. Miniver as they walked
towards the car, that one had boiled the milk for their bottles,
and washed their hands before lunch, and not let them eat
with a spoon which had been dropped on the floor.

Toby said suddenly, with a chuckle, 'We ought to have got
one for Teddy.' It would have been almost more bearable if
he had said it seriously. But just as they were getting into the
car a fat woman went past, with a fatter husband.

'You did look a fright,' she said. 'I 'ad to laugh.'

One had to laugh.

'Back to Normal'

' —— A ND a Welsh rabbit,' said Mrs. Miniver. 'Vin'll be spending the night here, and he likes that. Why, Mrs. Adie, what's the matter?'

'It's nothing, madam,' said Mrs. Adie, fumbling in vain for a handkerchief and finally wiping her eyes on her apron. 'It's only, it's so nice to be back to normal again.' A wintry smile re-established itself on her thin lips; she went out of the room, sniffing. It was the first sign of emotion she had shown since the Crisis began.

Back to normal. No, thought Mrs. Miniver, standing by the window and looking out into the square, they weren't quite back to normal, and never would be; none of them, except perhaps Toby. He was at an age when shapes, colours, and textures still meant more to him (as they do to some people throughout life) than human relationships. Therefore, his treasure was safe: there would always be warm moss and pink shells and smooth chestnuts. But the rest of them – even, to a slight degree, Judy – would never be exactly the same again. Richer and poorer, but not the same. Poorer by a few layers of security, by the sense of material permanence, by the conviction, when planting a bulb, that one would pretty certainly be there to see the daffodil in flower. But richer by several things, of which the most noticeable was a quickened eyesight. On the drive up from Starlings, a casual glimpse

through the window had reminded her of De La Mare's 'Fare
Well':—

> May the rusting harvest hedgerow
> Still the Traveller's Joy entwine
> And as happy children gather
>   Posies once mine.

And when things grew really serious – when Clem had gone
off with his Anti-Aircraft Battery, and Vin had been sent up
to Quern, and the children's day school had been evacuated to
the west country, and the maids had gone down to Starlings
to prepare it for refugees, and she herself, staying at her
sister's flat, had signed on as an ambulance driver – during all
the rather grim little bouts of staff-work which these arrangements entailed, she had been haunted day and night by the
next two lines of the same poem:—

> Look thy last on all things lovely
> Every hour. . . .

For even if none of them was killed or injured, and even if
their house did not, after all, attract one of the high-explosive
bombs intended for the near-by power station, yet these possibilities had been abruptly and urgently mooted: and they
had found themselves looking at each other, and at their cherished possessions, with new eyes. Small objects one could
send to the country – a picture or two, the second edition of
Donne, and the little antelope made of burnt jade; others, like
the furniture, one could more or less replace: but one could-
n't send away, or replace, the old panelling on the stairs, or the
one crooked pane in the dining-room window which made
the area railings look bent, or the notches on the nursery
door-post where they had measured the children every year.
And these, among their material belongings, were the ones
that had suddenly seemed to matter most.

Another thing they had gained was an appreciation of the value of dullness. As a rule, one tended to long for more drama, to feel that the level stretches of life between its high peaks were a waste of time. Well, there had been enough drama lately. They had lived through seven years in as many days; and Mrs. Miniver, at any rate, felt as though she had been wrung out and put through a mangle. She was tired to the marrow of her mind and heart, let alone her bones and ear-drums: and nothing in the world seemed more desirable than a long wet afternoon at a country vicarage with a rather boring aunt. A mountain range without valleys was merely a vast plateau, like the central part of Spain: and just about as exhausting to the nerves.

The third and most important gain was a sudden clarifying of intentions. On one of the blackest evenings of all several of their friends had dropped in to listen to the news and exchange plans. Among them were Badgecumbe, the old bio-chemist, and a young man called Flint, who wrote poetry and rather neat essays. When Mrs. Miniver switched off the set on a note of gloom they sat for a few moments too stunned to speak. Then Johnny Flint said:—

'I suppose that play of mine won't get written now. I've been talking about it for years. Oh, God. Nothing but a slim vol. and a bunch of light middles.'

And old Badger said in a tired growl from the depths of his armchair:—

'At least you'll still be young, Johnny, if you come through it at all. But I wish I'd left all the small stuff and concentrated on the I.P. experiments.'

'I know,' said Mrs. Miniver. 'I haven't got a pen like you, Johnny, or a laboratory like Badger. But there were a lot of things I wanted to do, too, that seemed fairly important. Only one never got around to them, somehow.'

'"Time's wingèd chariot,"' said Johnny bitterly. 'It's caught us up this time all right.'

'Looks like it,' said Mrs. Miniver. 'But if by any miraculous chance it *hasn't* . . .'

Well, it hadn't, after all. As she turned away from the
window the date on her writing-table calendar caught her
eye. Just a year ago, she remembered, she had stood at that
same window putting the summer away and preparing to
enjoy the autumn. And here she was again: only this time it
wasn't chrysanthemums she was rearranging, but values.

Badger and the Echidna

M RS. Miniver left the committee meeting about four o'clock in a mood half-way between exasperation and despair. The subject (a privately run, rather Utopian scheme connected with slum clearance) had fired her imagination when she had first heard of it: but why, she wondered, leaving the Comfreys' ample portico behind her and crossing over into Regent's Park, why must Pegasus always be harnessed to a dray, with a ham-handed cretin at the reins? By what mismanagement, what mistaking of bulk for importance, of bonhomie for goodwill, had a project like this been saddled with Lord Comfrey as chairman? And how could it succeed, if the meetings were always to be held in that moss-carpeted mausoleum of a house, at that smug post-prandial hour? If I had my way, she thought, walking very quickly so as to create a wind past her temples, I'd arrange the scene of every conference to suit its subject: and this particular committee ought to meet in a damp basement bedroom in Shoreditch, sitting on upturned soap-boxes. Rats, blackbeetles, and all.

She decided to go to the Zoo. It would be a relief to her feelings. As she passed the still open trenches she caught sight of old Badgecumbe standing among a little knot of sightseers, his vast head bent, his eyes hidden as usual beneath jutting, grizzled brows.

'Badger! You, rubber-necking?'

'I've been working with pyridine all day, and I need a breath of air.'

'So do I. Not pyridine – people. I was just going to do a Whitman. Why not come too?'

Badger nodded towards the trenches. 'Woolley and the rest of 'em dig to uncover past civilizations. We dig to bury our own.'

'I hear they're going to roof them in and put flower-beds on top.'

'Very suitable,' said Badger drily. 'To remind us, I suppose, that "this flower, safety," is still growing in pretty shallow soil.'

'Come *mee*-yer, Alf-ay!' A woman standing at the foot of a gravel mountain beckoned with peevish urgency to her child. 'You'll fall in and break your neck, and serve you right. And besides,' she added, 'you'll get them new boots in a muck.'

'"*I'm the King of the Castle*,"' chanted the urchin from the topmost pinnacle.

'I'll give you Castle . . .' She breasted the foot-hills briskly. But her son had already slithered to the ground on the other side, and was bearing down upon some new sightseers with outstretched palm.

'This wye to the trenches, lidy. Penny to show you round. . . .'

'I think perhaps you're right,' said Badger, taking Mrs. Miniver's arm. 'It'll be a relief to go and look at creatures who only behave grotesquely because they can't help it.'

'Let's choose the funniest,' said Mrs. Miniver. 'The mandrills. And the giraffes.'

They made their way towards the main entrance of the Zoo.

'On second thoughts,' said Badger, 'we'll go straight to the echidna. You know the echidna?'

'I've seen its cage, but it's never been actually on view.'

'It wouldn't be. It's nocturnal; but we'll get them to rout it out. It's worth seeing, as a horrible warning. *Zaglossus bruijnii*.

My unfavourite of God's creatures. If indeed it *is* one, which
I sometimes doubt.'

There was no gainsaying Badger. Mrs. Miniver relinquished
her hopes of the brilliant, sneering mandrills, the gentle,
bowing, improbable giraffes. But she liked the Small Rodent
House, anyway. It contained three of the most engaging animals
in the Zoo – the Indian Fruit Bat, which was like a doll's
umbrella; the Golden Hamster; and, best of all, the Fat Sand
Rat.

But Badger marched her straight past these to the low cages
at the end. The keeper opened the door of the sleeping-hutch;
and there, huddled in one corner, was what looked like a sack-
shaped lump of clay about two feet long. On closer
investigation, however, it proved to be covered with short,
sparse, dirty-white spines; and between the spines there was
some coarse greyish-brown hair. The keeper reached over and
lifted it out of the hutch by one hind leg. ('It's the only way,'
Badger explained. 'There's no other approach to an echidna.')
The under-side of the creature was even less attractive than its
top view. It had tiny pig's eyes, squeezed tightly shut. Its face,
almost non-existent, was extended into a pipe-shaped snout, so
long and thin that it looked far more like a tail than did the short
spatulate appendage at the other end of its body. Through this
snout, which it kept pressed down against its belly in a vain
attempt to curl up, it emitted a prolonged, petulant hissing. As
soon as the keeper put it down it hunched itself back into its
corner again, squirming with distaste for light and activity.

'Of course,' said Mrs. Miniver, trying to be fair, 'I suppose
it's more lively at night.'

'Not much,' said the keeper. 'Waddles out just far enough
to get its food, then back it goes.'

('Habitat: West End,' murmured Badger.)

'Sucks it in through that snout. No teeth.'

'Tell me,' said Mrs. Miniver, 'I see it's been here for a
good many years: have you ever managed to get up *any* affection for it?'

'Not much,' said the keeper, apologetically. 'It's just about alive, and that's all you can say for it.'

'Let's get out of here,' said Badger abruptly. 'It's as bad as pyridine. Besides, that animal gives me the horrors.'

'It's certainly not pretty,' said Mrs. Miniver.

'Pretty? It's criminal. It's what's been peopling half the world. Lowest sub-class of mammal. Barely alive. The incarnation of accidie.'

'Accidie? Oh, yes – one of the seven deadly sins.'

'The *only* deadly one,' said Badger. 'Well, here we've all been. Some of us less than others, but all of us to a certain extent. No vision. No energy. No discrimination. Spiritual monotremata.'

Mrs. Miniver had often noticed that when Badger got worked up his sentences grew shorter and his words longer. They stepped out into the fresh autumn sunshine.

A Wild Day

L OOKING up casually in the middle of writing a letter, Mrs.
Miniver saw, through the back window of the drawing-
room, something that she had never consciously seen before:
the last leaf being blown from a tree. One moment it was
there, on the highest bough of all, wagging wildly in the wind
and the rain. The next moment it was whirling away across
the roof tops, a forlorn ragged speck. The line of its flight was
the arabesque at the end of a chapter, the final scroll under
the death-warrant of summer. Once more the lime-tree stood
bone-naked.

So that was that: and a good thing, too. At first, like most
people, Mrs. Miniver had enjoyed the amazing spell of warm
weather which had lasted throughout October and most of
November. It had been pleasant and comforting; it had
helped to heal the scars which the last fortnight of September
had left behind. But later, as day after day broke close and
windless, and night after night failed to bring any refreshing
chill, she began to feel oddly uneasy. The year, now, seemed
like an ageing woman whose smooth cheeks were the result,
not of a heart perennially young, but of an assured income, a
sound digestion, and a protective callousness of spirit. Out of
those too-bright eyes there looked, now, not youthfulness,
but infantilism; and the smile which accompanied the look
was growing a little vacant.

Therefore, it had been a great relief when, a few days before, the weather had broken with a spectacular gale. The old beautiful painted aristocracy of the leaves, already tottering, had fallen in a night, overthrown by outward pressure and inward decadence. What remained were the essential masses of the tree, bare and sober, with a workaday beauty of their own. Through them, after a while, the sap would rise into a new aristocracy, which would flourish until it, too, had lost its freshness; and then fall. There is no other way, it seems, in a deciduous world. True evergreenness does not exist: the word is only another term for the ability to overlap the old with the new.

By the time she had finished her letter (which was a long one to Vin) the rain had nearly stopped, though the gale was as strong as ever. She put on a mackintosh and struggled up the square to the pillar-box. Outside the little newsagent's the evening paper placards were flapping under their wire grids like netted geese. The lower half of one of them had been folded upwards by the wind, hiding everything except the word 'JEWS.' Mrs. Miniver was conscious of an instantaneous mental wincing, and an almost instantaneous remorse for it. However long the horror continued, one must not get to the stage of refusing to think about it. To shrink from direct pain was bad enough, but to shrink from vicarious pain was the ultimate cowardice. And whereas to conceal direct pain was a virtue, to conceal vicarious pain was a sin. Only by feeling it to the utmost, and by expressing it, could the rest of the world help to heal the injury which had caused it. Money, food, clothing, shelter – people could give all these and still it would not be enough: it would not absolve them from the duty of paying in full, also, the imponderable tribute of grief.

She turned down the next street towards the river. It was Nannie's day out and she was going to fetch the children from school. The Royal Hospital, with bare straining trees in front of it and black flying clouds behind, stood sombrely magnificent, a fitting backcloth for the latest tragedy of the world. And here, perhaps, she thought as she battled along St. Leonard's Terrace under the lee of the wall, was a clue to the uneasiness which she had felt at the lingering on of summer. All the associations of November, the traditional flotsam left upon its shore by the successive tides of history, went ill with halcyon weather. It was the wind-month, the blood-month, Brumaire, the month of darkness: its sign was the evil scorpion, who, when surrounded by a ring of fire, was said to sting itself and die of its own poison. It was ushered in by the Vigil of Saman, Lord of Death, by the witches and warlocks of Hallowe'en. A later tide had left a later mark – the ritual bonfires of Guy Fawkes' Day, round which children still stood in primitive excitement, their innocent eyes reflecting unconsciously the twin flames of sadism and fire-worship. This year, down at Starlings, the farmer's children next door had made an extra large bonfire, and for the Guy's face they had used a mask representing the wicked Queen out of Disney's 'Seven Dwarfs,' which Joey Iggulsden had bought at the village shop. This blend of two nursery ideologies, three hundred years apart, had particularly appealed to Clem. It showed, he said, that children had an inborn knowledge that evil was evil, irrespective of time or place: but Vin said it only showed that Joey Iggulsden had a sense of humour. Anyway, it had been a grand bonfire, of a terrifying heat and redness. Mrs. Miniver had tried for a few moments to treat the scene as a reality, and had found herself wondering whether there was any cause or conviction in the world for which she would have the courage to go to the stake. She could think of several for which she would make the attempt: but, as the effigy lurched forward suddenly from the waist, with forked flames writhing out of its sleeves like burning fingers, and its painted leer crumpling up in the heat, she shuddered, and admitted humbly enough that she herself would probably recant at the crackling of the first twig.

However, nobody nowadays was burnt at the stake. The unfortunate ones of the world were subjected to a more lingering torment, and the fortunate ones were merely condemned to watch it from a front seat, unwilling *tricoteuses* at an execution they were powerless to prevent. The least they could do was not to turn away their eyes; for with such a picture stamped upon the retina of their memory they would not be able to lie easy until they had done their best to ensure that it could never happen again. But it was going to leave yet another ineffaceable watermark on the bleak shores of November.

When she reached the Embankment she met the full force of the gale, and exulted in it. Yes, this was the kind of weather that the events of the world called for: a wild, dark day, suitable for a wild, dark mood. From the two tall chimneys of the power station the smoke streamed out horizontally, a black banner and a white one. The river was at the three-quarter flood. It looked like a battlefield, water and wind meeting angrily in a thousand small hand-to-hand contests. But in an hour or so the tide would turn.

New Year's Eve

NEW Year's Eve was the only day of the year on which Mrs. Adie really unbent. Christmas she held to be of little account, though she cooked the turkey and the mince-pies faithfully enough and took a benign interest in the children's presents. Boxing Day made her, if anything, more tight-lipped than usual, for on that day the Minivers were in the habit of eating a 'June dinner' as a respite from Christmas food: a practice which Mrs. Adie looked upon as unnatural and faintly sacrilegious. There was a no-good-can-come-of-this expression on her face as she served up the clear soup, the fish mayonnaise, and the summer pudding (made of bottled currants and raspberries); but up till now nobody had so much as choked on a fish-bone.

On New Year's Eve, however, Mrs. Adie always invited the whole family into the kitchen for a Hogmanay tea. There were scones and oatcakes and shortbread and rowan jelly; and a Melrose sponge-cake sent down by her brother, and a Selkirk bannock sent down by her sister; and in addition to all these she managed to provide a constant supply of fresh drop-scones all through the meal. She let the children take turns in pouring spoonfuls of batter on to the hot girdle, and in watching each little sizzling yellow pool go beautifully brown round the edges. She even let Gladys make a few, on condition that she gave up her regrettable Sassenach habit of calling them 'flapjacks.'

After tea came an even greater treat – the fortune-telling. Clem and Vin pushed the table back, and they all settled down round the kitchen fire, while Mrs. Adie produced a large iron saucepan, seven bowls of cold water, and a box full of pieces of lead which she had somehow collected during the past twelve months from various sources, such as plumbers and roof-menders. (At this time of year Vin always took care to lock up the cupboard in which his sea-fishing tackle was kept: he was afraid that Mrs. Adie might have her eye on the weights.)

While the lead was still melting in the saucepan the children were allowed to peer over it and watch. But when all the dull grey lumps had dissolved into a pool of liquid silver Mrs. Adie made everybody move back to a safe distance. Then she arranged the seven bowls of water in a row on the hearth, pulled on a pair of old leather gauntlets, lifted the pan off the fire, and poured a generous dollop of lead into each bowl. The noise it made as it entered the water was peculiar, and rather frightening – something between the crack of a pistol-shot and the hiss of an angry swan. Toby always blocked his ears and stood very close to Clem; and Gladys, who was new to this ceremony, gave a shrill 'Oo!' and retreated into the scullery.

'C'm mout o' there,' said Mrs. Adie contemptuously. 'It'll not hurt you. If you run from your lead you'll run from your luck.'

Obedient to the power of rhythm and alliteration, Gladys came back. Marvellous, thought Mrs. Miniver, the way almost any Scot, in almost any situation, can coin a phrase which has the authentic ring and cogency of an ancient proverb.

And now Mrs. Adie knelt down on the hearth, took off her gloves, fished the bright silvery 'fortunes' out of the water, and began to interpret them. The lead had hardened into the most fantastic shapes: shapes like groups of statuary, like fern-fronds, like intricate machinery, like outstretched wings, like gnarled olive-trees. To the uninitiated, they might have meant anything or nothing; but Mrs. Adie – helped, it is true, by a pretty close knowledge of her hearers – contrived to give each of them a detailed and appropriate meaning.

'My word now!' she would say, speaking to Judy but at Clem, because it was easier that way, 'look at all these fine new houses your daddy's going to be architecting. And one of them's got a terrible tall tower to it – aye, it'll be a kirk he's to build next, sure enough.' And then, to Vin: 'Here's you with a fishing-rod in your hand and a great big fish on the other end of it and a wheen more o' them lying round about your feet. Oh, it's going to be a grand year for the fishing, and no mistake.' And to Toby: 'Now there's two wee wheels in this one, as plain as plain. That'll be that bicycle you're wanting for your birthday, my lamb. . . . And whatever's this I can see in yours, Nannie? My lands! I believe it's a wedding-cake!'

'It's no such thing,' said Nannie primly. 'It's a nice big new work-basket, that's what it is. Just the thing I need, with the amount of stockings they all manage to wear out down here.'

'Well, well, we'll see,' said Mrs. Adie darkly. 'Wedding-cake or work-basket, what will be will be, and one thing leads to another.'

There she goes again, thought Mrs. Miniver with an inward chuckle. Rhythm and alliteration: the phrase-makers always get the last word. She herself was sitting in a big wicker armchair at one side of the range. She had drawn back a little because of the heat, and from where she sat, half in shadow, the scene looked wonderfully theatrical. Mrs. Adie, with a flush on her high cheek-bones and her usually neat hair quite dishevelled, was reaching forward to fish out Judy's 'fortune'; and, opposite, the six fire-lit faces were awaiting, with varying degrees of credulity, her next pronouncement. It didn't much matter, after all, whether the fortunes came true, or whether anybody believed in them; what mattered was that here at least was one small roomful of warmth and happiness, shut in by frail window-panes from a freezing, harsh, and inexplicable world. All one could do was to be thankful for moments like these. During the next twelve months, perhaps, the remaining odds and ends of their civilization would have been tipped into the melting-pot; and not even Mrs. Adie—

But she became aware that her own fortune had just been told out of the seventh bowl and that she had not heard a word of it.

'Thank you so much, Mrs. Adie,' she said with a smile, taking the cold, queer-shaped lump of metal on to her palm. So far as she could remember, it was almost exactly the same shape as the one she had had last year. So that was all right: for herself, she could think of nothing better.

Choosing a Doll

I T was Judy's birthday. For some reason, her presents this year included an unusually large proportion of money. There were several postal orders, a half-crown or two, a ten-shilling note from Clem's father, and fourpence-halfpenny from Toby, who had bought her a purse as a present and thoughtfully put into it everything that he happened to have got left. Altogether it came to nearly thirty shillings, which was an unprecedented amount.

Judy had long ago discovered that the chief problem about spending present-money was to choose between quality and quantity; between the satisfaction of buying something really worth while, far beyond the scope of her weekly allowance, and the excitement of returning home with an armful of smaller parcels: so she had worked out a form of compromise which she called Crust and Crumb. This time she decided to lay out about fifteen shillings on Crust, in the shape of a new doll, and to spend the rest later on Crumb. So the day after her birthday she persuaded her mother to come on a shopping expedition.

The choice of a doll, Judy found, was unexpectedly difficult. They were things you didn't usually get a chance to choose for yourself: they arrived as presents, chosen for you by other people, and you had to get to know them and love them as they were. But when you saw rows and rows of them together it was almost impossible to be sure which you liked best. She explained this to her mother.

'You see, it would be so awful to pick the wrong one. I mean, suppose you could have gone and bought me in a shop instead of just having me; you might have made a mistake and chosen Marigold Thompson instead.'

Mrs. Miniver's mouth twitched. She couldn't somehow imagine herself choosing Marigold Thompson. A nice child, but pudding-faced.

'Well,' she said, 'I like Marigold.'

'Oh, so do I. But what I mean is, she wouldn't have done for *you*. And what's more,' pursued Judy, 'Marigold's mother wouldn't have done for me. At all,' she added with conviction.

'Why don't you like Marigold's mother?' asked Mrs. Miniver. 'She's always very kind to you. And she's frightfully fond of children.'

'Oh, I know. She told me so. But you see, when people are frightfully fond of children you never know whether they really like *you* or not, do you?'

Mrs. Miniver felt a quick glow of sympathy. It was exactly what she had so often thought about the boringness of the sort of man who 'likes women.'

'And besides,' Judy went on, 'she makes such a Thing about everything, if you know what I mean.'

Mrs. Miniver knew only too well. She had been at school with Marigold's mother.

'And do you happen to know,' she asked, 'what Marigold thinks of me?'

'Oh, she likes you,' said Judy. 'She says you leave people alone.'

Mrs. Miniver cast her mind back, trying to remember whether she and her contemporaries had discussed one another's parents so freely and with such perception. Not till much later, she felt sure – fourteen or fifteen, perhaps; at Judy's age one had more or less taken them for granted, comparing them only in degree of strictness. And to discuss them with one's own parents would have been quite impossible: horizontal divisions were far stronger in those days than vertical ones. Perhaps the psychologists were right, and the 'child mind' – that convenient abstraction – matured earlier nowadays. On the other hand, she herself had outgrown dolls by the age of nine, and here was Judy, at eleven, buying a new one.

One thing was certain: the ultra-modern dolls, with felt features realistically modelled, had no appeal for Judy at all. Mrs. Miniver, quite early in the expedition, had pointed one of them out. 'Look, it's exactly like a real child – isn't it lovely?'

'Oh, no!' said Judy with unexpected vehemence. 'I don't like it at all. You see, it's not in the least like a real *doll*.' And she turned away again to the ringlets, the huge eyes, and the tiny rose-bud mouths. It was odd, thought her mother: dolls, which had begun by being crude imitations of men and women, had ended by developing a racial type of their own; and now apparently they could not stray from this without becoming less lovable.

Judy eventually managed to narrow her field of choice down to two – a blonde in blue silk and a brunette in pink organdie; but between these she was quite unable to decide. 'Better toss up,' said her mother at last. They tossed with Toby's halfpenny, and the blonde doll won. Judy stood staring at the two open boxes, her eyes round with surprise.

'Mummy, how extraordinary! I thought I liked them both exactly the same, but now I know for certain it's the dark one I want. Have *you* ever noticed that about tossing up?'

'Often,' said Mrs. Miniver, smiling. She remembered with what astonishment, in her own childhood, she had stumbled upon that particular piece of knowledge; and reflected once more how much of the fun of parenthood lay in watching the children remake, with delighted wonder, one's own discoveries.

At the Dentist's

'QUITE comfortable?' asked Mr. Hinchley when he had played his usual little overture upon the various pedals and handles of his adjustable chair.

'Quite, thank you,' said Mrs. Miniver. Horribly, she felt inclined to add. For really it was the refinement of civilized cruelty, this spick, span, and ingenious affair of shining leather and gleaming steel, which hoisted you and tilted you and fitted reassuringly into the small of your back and cupped your head tenderly between padded cushions. It ensured for you a more complete muscular relaxation than any armchair that you could buy for your own home: but it left your tormented nerves without even the solace of a counter-irritant. In the old days the victim's attention had at least been distracted by an ache in the back, a crick in the neck, pins and needles in the legs, and the uneasy tickling of plush under the palm. But now, too efficiently suspended between heaven and earth, you were at liberty to concentrate on hell.

'A *lit*-tle wider,' said Mr. Hinchley indulgently, dividing the words into separate syllables as though he were teaching a very small child to read. He was a kind, brisk, blond young man who smelt (thank heaven) of nothing except rather good shaving-soap. Mrs. Miniver obeyed meekly and resigned herself to the exquisite discomfort of the electric drill. It was a pity, she felt, that this instrument had been invented during a period when scientific images in poetry were out of favour. To the moderns, who had been brought up with it, it was presumably *vieux jeu*. They took it for granted; it did not fire their imagination like the pylons and the power-houses which were now the fashionable emotive symbols. But oh, what Donne could have made of it, if it had been invented in his time! With what delight he would have seized upon it, with what harsh jostling and grinding of consonants he would have worked out metaphor after metaphor, comparing its action to that of all the worst tormentors of the heart: to jealousy, to remorse, to the sharp gnawing of a bad conscience and the squalid nagging of debt.

'Are you quite all right?' Mr. Hinchley inquired solicitously.

'*Eye* aw eye,' said Mrs. Miniver. Oh, *quite* all right Grand. I love it. This is just my idea of the way to spend a fine afternoon in early spring. For early spring it undoubtedly was, even though there might be a chunk of late winter still to come. Although they were not yet in bud, the bare trees outside Mr. Hinchley's window had a quickened, bloomy look like the expression on the face of somebody who has just had a good idea but has not yet put it into words; and the sky behind them was as clearly, flatly blue as the sky in an aunt's water-colour. Mrs. Miniver kept her eyes focused as long as possible upon the far distance, hoping that they would take her other senses with them. But they didn't. The drill was too insistent. So presently she brought them back and cast a reproachful spaniel-glance upwards at Mr. Hinchley, which he was too much absorbed to see. She devoted the next few minutes to making a slow, dispassionate study of his left eyebrow, which was a good enough shape as eyebrows go; and then decided that nothing but a deep romantic love could make the human face tolerable at such close quarters.

The far and the near having both failed her, she explored the middle distance: the embossed plaster patterns on the ceiling; the round, white lamp – an albino moon – which hung between her and the window; the X-ray machine; the sterilizer; the glass bowl on her left with the tumbler of pink mouth-wash beside it; and on her right the large composite fitment, so absurdly like a porcelain snowman, out of which burgeoned, among other things, this insufferable, this inescapable, this altogether abominable drill.

'Don't forget,' said Mr. Hinchley brightly, 'you can always switch it off yourself if it gets unpleasant.'

'Ank,' said Mrs. Miniver. *Gets* unpleasant. . . . Understatement could be carried too far. She felt with her forefinger for the small cold knob on the right arm of the chair, which would, if she pressed it, silence the monster at once. This, at any rate, was a humane provision which did not exist in the case of jealousy and the other tormentors. But so far as Mrs. Miniver was concerned it might just as well not have been there, for she had never yet been able to bring herself to use it. Something always held her back – some vague blend of noble and ignoble motives, of pride and masochism and *noblesse oblige* and the Spartan Boy and Kate Barlass and a quite unreasonable feeling of hostility towards the white-veiled, white-coated young woman who hovered all the time behind Mr. Hinchley waiting for him to say 'Double-ended spatula' or 'Pink wax.' There was nothing whatever wrong with Miss Bligh, who was civil, decorative, and efficient: but somehow her presence made the use of the merciful switch a psychological impossibility.

And now, at last, Mr. Hinchley turned off the drill of his own accord.

'Finished?' asked Mrs. Miniver with a hopeful, lopsided smile.

'Afraid not. But I thought you'd had about as much as you could do with. I'd better give you a local.'

Miss Bligh, as though by prestidigitation, suddenly held a syringe between her scarlet finger-tips. She could just as easily, Mrs. Miniver felt, have produced a billiard ball, a white rabbit, or an ace-high straight flush. The prick of the injection was sharp, but its effect was magical. In an instant the left-hand side of her face ceased to belong to her. She put up one finger and stroked her cheek curiously. It was like stroking somebody else's; and therefore it was, tactually, like seeing herself clearly for the first time. Not in a mirror, where the eyes must always bear the double burden of looking and being looked into; but from outside, through a window, catching herself in profile and unawares.

Oh! page John Donne, she thought again impatiently. Run, buttoned cherubim, through the palm lounges and gilt corridors of heaven, turning his name (as is your habit) into a falling, drawling dissyllable. '*Meess*-tah *Dah*-ahnne . . . *Meess*-tah *Dah*-ahnne . . .' And tell him that there are at least two poems waiting to be written in Mr. Hinchley's surgery. Miss Bligh will hand him a pen.

A Pocketful of Pebbles

As she walked past a cab rank in Pont Street Mrs. Miniver
heard a very fat taxi-driver with a bottle nose saying to a
very old taxi-driver with a rheumy eye: 'They say it's all a
question of your subconscious mind.'

Enchanted, she put the incident into her pocket for Clem.
It jostled, a bright pebble, against several others: she had had
a rewarding day. And Clem, who had driven down to the
country to lunch with a client, would be pretty certain to
come back with some good stuff, too. This was the cream of
marriage, this nightly turning out of the day's pocketful of
memories, this deft habitual sharing of two pairs of eyes, two
pairs of ears. It gave you, in a sense, almost a double life:
though never, on the other hand, quite a single one.

She found herself involuntarily rehearsing her pebble as
she walked. 'It was pure *New Yorker*. Just as I went past, the
fat one said to the old one . . .' And then it would be Clem's
turn: 'There was a superb horsy man there, like a prawn with
a regimental tie. He said: "What I always say is, there's gone
in the wind and – er – gone in the wind."' And then she could
bring out Mary's engagement, heard of by telephone after
Clem had left the house; and the joke which Toby had made
on the way to school; and, best of all, a beautiful saga about
the woman who had sat next to her at lunch. Mrs. Miniver
had not heard her name at all, but if she had invented her she

would have called her Burfish. Lady Constance Burfish, probably: or perhaps Mrs. Claude Burfish would be subtler. Anyway, it appeared that she lived in Gloucestershire: where did Mrs. Miniver live? In London, but they had a small house in Kent.

'In Kent? How nice,' said Mrs. Burfish. Her tone conveyed that Kent was not quite out of the top drawer.

The talk turned, inevitably, on to the evacuation and billeting of children. Mrs. Miniver said they had offered to take six at Starlings, or more if the Government would provide enough beds to turn the oast-house playroom into a dormitory.

'Wonderful of you,' said Mrs. Burfish. 'But, you know, a small house *is* rather different. I mean, one doesn't expect – does one? – to keep up *quite* the same standards. . . .'

Mrs. Miniver, whose standards of comfort, like Clem's, were almost reprehensibly high, mentally compared the compact warmth of Starlings with some of the bedrooms she had occupied in large country houses. But she said nothing: she did not want to interrupt what promised to be an enjoyable turn.

'Of course,' went on Mrs. Burfish (no, she would have to be Lady Constance after all), 'I was perfectly *civil* to the little woman they sent round. In fact, I felt quite sorry for her. I said: "What an unpleasant job it must be for you, having to worm your way into people's houses like this." But you know, she didn't seem to mind. I suppose some people aren't very sensitive.'

'No,' said Mrs. Miniver, 'I suppose not.'

'And I said to her quite plainly, "*If* there's a war you'll find me only too willing to do my duty. But I *cannot* see the point," I said, "of tying oneself down publicly beforehand and upsetting the servants."'

What luck I do have, thought Mrs. Miniver gratefully. She had, of course, read about this kind of thing in the papers, but a friend of hers who had helped with the billeting survey had assured her that it was mercifully rare. So that now, face to face – or rather, elbow to elbow – with an authentic example of it, she was filled with the same sense of privileged awe which had overcome her when, emerging suddenly from a painful encounter with a juniper thicket in Teesdale, she had once seen a startled woodcock unmistakably carrying off its young between its feet. Looking, fascinated, at Lady Constance, she almost felt that she ought to write a letter to *The Field*. Moreover, Lady Constance seemed bent upon giving good measure. For she went on:—

'And, of course, I said to her before she left: "Even if the worst does come to the worst, you must make it quite clear to the authorities that I can only accept Really Nice Children."'

'And where,' Mrs. Miniver could not restrain herself from asking, 'are the other ones to go?'

'There are sure to be camps,' said Lady Constance firmly.

The talk swung in the opposite direction. A few minutes later Mrs. Miniver heard Lady Constance's other neighbour, who bore one of the famous Norfolk surnames, saying politely: 'In Gloucestershire? How nice.'

Kent was avenged.

Brambles and Apple-trees

'THE worst of gardening,' said Mrs. Miniver, lying along one of the upper boughs of an apple-tree and reaching out to snip with a satisfying crunch through a half-inch-thick bramble, 'is that it's so full of metaphors one hardly knows where to begin.'

'I know,' said Clem from the ground below. He severed the root of the bramble with a bill-hook and began to haul it down hand over hand like a rope. 'This is a prize one. It must have been about thirty feet long when it was whole.'

They had just bought the tiny white weather-boarded cottage on the far side of Starlings Wood, which had been standing empty ever since old Parsloe, the hurdle-maker, had died there a year ago. For at least two years before that he had been almost bedridden, so that the little garden and orchard had become a wilderness. The Minivers had bought it partly because they were afraid that Bateman, the local builder, might get hold of it first and spoil it, and partly because, having made Starlings as nearly perfect as they could, they were both filled with a restless longing for new material: a state of mind which is as natural in the sphere of house-property as it is in that of human relationships, but which those who do not share it are apt to mistake for inconstancy. Of this there was no question, for they both adored Starlings and would not have exchanged it for any other house in

England: but just at the moment they were frankly enjoying a
pretty shameless flirtation with old Parsloe's cottage. When it
was finished, as Clem said, they would probably marry it off
to one of their friends; in the meanwhile it was the making of
the Easter holidays. They came over with the children nearly
every day, working indoors when the weather was bad, and
out of doors when it was fine: painting and whitewashing
and carpentering and digging and weeding and planting,
without too deeply inquiring why, and for whom, they were
doing it.

Beyond the potato-patch, close under the high-banked
hedge which separated the garden from Carter's Lane, there
stood three apple-trees. These, during the last few years, had
been stealthily but steadily invaded by an army of brambles.
Some had pressed downwards from the bank in a solid pha-
lanx, smothering the hinder branches almost to death; others
had thrust upwards from the ground, looping themselves
over the topmost boughs and falling to take root again on the
other side, so that the trees were bound to the earth with
criss-cross cords, like haystacks on a windy headland. The
job of rescuing them – combining as it did all the most
attractive features of a crusade and a demolition contract –
was one which the Minivers particularly enjoyed.
Constructive destruction is one of the most delightful
employments in the world, and in civilized life the opportu-
nities for it are only too rare. Also, a bonfire is always fun;
and here was an excellent excuse for the children to keep one
going all day and every day, piling it high with Clem's big
bramble-faggots and roasting potatoes (very unevenly) in the
intervals. As for Mrs. Miniver herself, she only regretted
that circumstances had never led her to discover that the way
to spend the spring was up an apple-tree, in daily intimacy
with its bark, leaves, and buds. In early spring, as in the early
years of children, there are times when the clock races, the
film runs in swift motion, and the passionate watcher does
not dare to glance away for fear he should miss some lovely

and fleeting phase. The present week was one of those times. She looked, and the buds were as tightly, rosily clenched as a baby's fist; she looked again, and they were half uncurled. To-morrow they would be nearly open; the next day, perhaps, in full bloom, like those of the pear-tree on the other side of the garden, which towered up in the sunlight as tall, rounded and dazzling as a cumulus cloud.

'Time for beer,' said Clem, and went into the cottage to get it.

Mrs. Miniver stuck her secateurs into her belt and disposed herself more comfortably among the branches. She was determined not to come down to earth before she need; if possible, never. Peering downwards through the young leaves, she could see Toby making an elaborate entanglement with twigs and cotton over some newly sown grass. He trod on the seeds a good deal, because his soul was bent on getting the pattern of the network symmetrical. Vin and Judy were eating potatoes and racing snails up the gate-posts. In the field beyond, two lambs – the only living creatures which never fail to come up to expectation – were authentically gambolling. Their whiteness rivalled the pear-blossom's. The smoke of the bonfire drifted, blue and sweet, across the potato-patch. An invisible, indefatigable blackbird went on saying 'Doh-mi!' from somewhere on the other side of Carter's Lane; he had made this remark so many hundreds of times every day that they were all beginning to ignore it.

Clem, coming out of the cottage, paused for a moment to take a critical look at what they had done.

'We've made a lot of difference to-day,' he said, as he handed her glass up to her through the branches. 'One is really beginning to see the shape of the trees.'

'I suppose,' said Mrs. Miniver between gulps, 'the brambles would try to make out that the apple-trees had been practising encirclement.'

'That reminds me,' said Clem. 'We ought to be getting home pretty soon if we don't want to be late for the news.'

The Khelim Rug

'PROFESSOR Badgecumbe has just telephoned to say that he is very sorry indeed, but he can't get back for another twenty minutes.' Behind his secretary's air of apology crouched a protecting tigress, ready to spring if Mrs. Miniver showed the least sign of vexation. To Miss Perrin Badger was a god, and luncheon guests whom he kept waiting had no right whatever to complain. The privilege of knowing him ought to be enough for them.

'It doesn't matter in the least,' said Mrs. Miniver, who rather agreed with her. 'I'm sure he must have been unavoidably detained.'

'I'm sure he must.' The tigress relaxed, mollified.

Unavoidably detained my foot, thought Mrs. Miniver. He had probably been messing about in his laboratory and had simply forgotten the time; or else he had been struck by a brilliant new idea in the Tube and had been carried on to the terminus. She knew this perfectly well, and so did Miss Perrin, and each knew that the other knew it. But they both loved Badger: so the Professor was unavoidably detained, and Mrs. Miniver sat down to wait in his study.

As a matter of fact she was glad. She had been living for several weeks through one of those arid stretches of life which lie here and there between its more rewarding moments; where there is neither nobility nor gaiety, neither civic splendour nor country peace, but only allotments and rubbish-tips, the gas-works on one side and a row of dilapidated hoardings on the other. As a rule she managed to keep household matters in what she considered their proper place. They should be no more, she felt, than a low, unobtrusive humming in the background of consciousness: the mechanics of life should never be allowed to interfere with living. But every now and then some impish poltergeist seemed to throw a spanner into the works. Everything went wrong at once: chimneys smoked, pipes burst, vacuum-cleaners fused, china and glass fell to pieces, net curtains disintegrated in the wash. Nannie sprained her ankle, the cook got tonsilitis, the house-parlourmaid left to be married, and the butterfly nut off the mincing-machine was nowhere to be found.

At such times, she knew, you must just put on spiritual dungarees and remain in them until things are running smoothly again. Every morning you awake to the kind of list which begins:— *Sink-plug. Ruffle-tape. X-hooks. Glue . . .* and ends:— *Ring plumber. Get sweep. Curse laundry.* Your horizon contracts, your mind's eye is focused upon a small circle of exasperating detail. Sterility sets in; the hatches of your mind are battened down. Your thoughts, once darling companions, turn into club bores, from which only sleep can bring release. When you are in this state, to be kept waiting for half an hour in somebody else's house is nothing but the purest joy. At home the footstool limps, legless, thirsting for its glue; the curtain material lies virginally unruffled; the laundry, unconscious of your displeasure, dozes peacefully at Acton: while you yourself are free. Yet you have not played truant: truancy has been thrust upon you, thanks to the fact that elderly professors so obligingly live up to their reputation for absent-mindedness.

She leant back in Badger's armchair and prepared to let her mind stray wherever it liked. But it had got into spiritless habits, like a dog which has been kept on a lead, and for several minutes it would do nothing but potter about sniffing at the kind of object it had grown accustomed to. There was a handle, it informed her, missing from Badger's desk; the bookcase had a cracked pane, and the glass finger-plate on the door was hanging by a single screw. Look here, said Mrs. Miniver, haven't I had enough of this sort of thing lately? Run away and bring me something interesting. That's what any decent mind ought to do for its owner when she lets it off the leash – just go bounding away into the long grass and bring back a really profound thought, laying it at her feet all furry and palpitating. C'mon, now. *Hey los'!*

Her gaze wandered to the floor. The hearth-rug was an old Khelim strip, threadbare but still glowing. Its border was made up of a row of small lozenges, joined by their acute angles. Beginning on the extreme left, she let her eye run idly along this row, naming the colours to herself as she came to them. *Blue, purple, red. Blue, purple, re*— but here she was checked, for the second red was different from the first. So she had to begin again. *Blue, purple, scarlet. Blue, purple, crimson. Blue, purple, sc*— but here was yet a third red, which made the first one look almost orange. *Blue, purple, flame*, then. *Blue, purple, crimson. Blue, purple, scarlet.* . . .

And this, it occurred to her, is one of the things that make life so difficult. The linked experiences of which it is composed appear to you one at a time; it is therefore impossible to gauge their relative significance. In how much detail ought you to notice each one before it slips into the past? Will 'red' do, or must you cudgel your brains for a more exact description, hesitating between claret and magenta, vermilion and cardinal? This grief, that joy, this interview, that relationship, this motor-smash, that picnic – can you weigh it up once for all and assign to it a fixed position in your scale of memories, or will you sooner or later be forced to take it out again and reclassify it? This dusty and tedious little patch of time – could she safely label it 'drab' and have done with it, or would she find herself one day living through a period so relentlessly subfusc that this present lozenge would seem, by contrast, gay?

The door opened and Badger came in. His beard arrived first, his eyebrows next, then the rest of his vast yet twinkling bulk.

'I'm afraid I'm a little late,' he said. It was five minutes past two.

On the River

'WATER-RAT,' said Vin, jerking his head in the direction of the bank. His mother looked round just in time to see the bright eyes and sleek furry body before it disappeared behind a clump of reeds.

'Oof!' said Clem. 'Let's take it a bit easier. You're in train-ing and I'm not. I'd forgotten how far it was to Aunt Hetty's by river.'

'It's only about a mile now,' said Vin, slacking off a little. Mrs. Miniver, lying back and trailing one hand in the water, wondered what Vin thought of, consciously or subcon-sciously, when he said the word 'mile.' Probably the stretch of road between the house and the village at his grandfather's; that was where they had spent most of their summer holidays when he was small, before they bought Starlings. 'It's just a mile to the post office,' somebody was certain to have said in his hearing: so that from then onwards, for the rest of his life, all his miles would be measured against that one. Judy's private mile, most likely, was the cart-track through the fields from Starlings to Brickwall Farm – her favourite walk. Toby's might be this, too, eventually, but Toby was not yet mile-conscious. He still measured his distances by true and not by artificial reckoning: he knew quite well that Brickwall Farm was a long way off when you were tired and no distance at all when you weren't. It was the same with time. 'Ten minutes,' for Mrs. Miniver herself, would always mean the length of the mid-morning break in her lessons with her first governess; and 'an hour' was the formal time after tea in her grandmother's drawing-room, in a clean frock and sash.

Aunt Hetty was sitting in her summer-house at the water's edge, knitting a sock and keeping a look-out for them. They moored the boat at her little landing-stage and stepped ashore.

'My dears! Lovely to see you,' said Aunt Hetty, rolling up her wool and impaling the ball on her needles as though she was skewering a piece of mutton to make a *shashlik*. 'Come along – we're having tea in the strawberry-bed.'

'*In* the strawberry-bed?'

'Yes. It's a new idea that occurred to me last time Vin was here. You know how much better they always taste when you eat them straight off the plants? Only the drawback is, there's never any cream and sugar. So I thought, why not take the cream and sugar under the nets with us? We tried it, and it's a capital plan. I can't imagine why I never thought of it before.' She took Vin's arm and led the way across the lawn. The others followed, exchanging telegraphically, with a smile, their amused affection for Aunt Hetty. Glorious woman: nobody else would have had an idea like that – or rather, nobody else would have put it seriously and efficiently into practice, complete with table, chairs, silver tea-pot, and cucumber sandwiches. She had even had the nets heightened on poles to give more head-room.

When tea was over, Vin took Clem off to show him the place where he had hooked (but lost) a monster trout the week before. With any luck, he said, it might still be there.

'Sure to be,' said Clem. 'I don't mind betting it's the same one *I* used to see. They're immortal, these Thames trout.'

Mrs. Miniver and Aunt Hetty strolled down to the summer-house again.

'My supply of great-nephews is running low,' said Aunt Hetty, unskewering the *shashlik*. 'Margaret's youngest boy leaves at the end of this half, and then I shall only have Vin. And when *he* leaves, I suppose there'll be a two years' gap before Toby comes.'

'I'm afraid so. Although from a financial point of view that's rather a relief.'

Aunt Hetty snorted.

'From an aunt's point of view it's unpardonable. Between the lot of you, you ought to have arranged things better. What on earth d'you think I'm here for, I should like to know?'

To be a pattern and example to all aunts, thought Mrs. Miniver; to be a delight to boys and a comfort to their parents; and to show that at least one daughter in every generation ought to remain unmarried, raise the profession of auntship to a fine art, and make a point of having a house within the five-mile limit, preferably between Boveney and Queen's Eyot.

Aunt Hetty threw a piece of cake to a swan. She always brought some down for them after tea.

'Not that I like swans,' she admitted. 'But they're one's neighbours, and I think it's best to keep in with them.'

'I know. Conceited brutes. They always look as though they'd just been reading their own fan-mail.'

It was not long before the others came back. They had seen the trout, and Clem swore that it had looked up and given him a leer of recognition.

'We'll have to be going,' said Vin regretfully. 'There isn't a Queen's Eyot Absence to-day, worse luck.'

Looking back as they rounded the next bend of the river, they could see Aunt Hetty still waving good-bye to them, sock in hand, the sun glinting on her needles.

It had been a lovely afternoon, thought Mrs. Miniver as they moved smoothly downstream between the low green banks. In most parts of England this was the season of the year that she liked the least – this ripe, sultry time when the trees were no longer jade but malachite, and the hedges looked almost black against the pale parched fields. In the country round Starlings, especially, spring was the real apex of the year. Summer was bathos, *dégringolade*: one waited longingly for autumn, which would bring back colour and magic. But in this sort of landscape, high summer was the perfect time. Here, the grass of the water-meadows was fresh, cool, and green; the steady onward sweep of the river, the quivering reflections in its depths and the play of light on its surface, gave movement and variety, so that one felt none of that brooding stillness which mars July in unwatered countrysides. Even the rank and ramping vegetation of summer (such a come-down, in most places, after the delicate miraculous experiments of spring) seemed here to be superbly appropriate, like large jewellery on a fine, bold, handsome woman. Down by the water's edge there were coarse clumps of comfrey and fig-wort, hemp agrimony and giant dock; on the banks, a tangle of vetch and convolvulus, moon-daisies, yarrow, and bedstraw; while from higher up still came the heavy, heady sweetness of elder flowers.

'Gosh!' said Vin suddenly, after a long spell of silence. 'Long Leave's the end of next week. This half seems to have gone most frightfully quick.'

'Summer halves do,' said Clem.

Left and Right

THE conversation at dinner had been so heated that by the end of it Mrs. Miniver had developed mental, moral, and physical indigestion. Teresa Frant, usually a brilliant mixer of unlikely human ingredients, had experimented for once a little too boldly. Or perhaps (for one never knew with Teresa) she had done it out of mischief. She had never had any use for her rich diehard sister-in-law Agnes Lingfield; but if she really wanted to bait her she could have chosen a more effective, because less far-fetched, opponent than little Neish. For in addition to the personal antipathy which had struck almost visible sparks from their finger-tips at the moment of introduction, these two people were so irrevocably separated by race, class, age, sex, religion, politics, and cast of mind that it seemed absurd to classify them both as human beings. The zoo authorities had clearly put one or the other of them into the wrong cage. Therefore the argument which had sprung up between them during dinner had ended by being not so much a duel as a brawl: and while duels with food are both entertaining and eupeptic, brawls are neither.

It began by Lady Lingfield turning to Neish and saying through impalpable lorgnettes, 'I hear you're one of these Layba people: I've always wondered what it *feels* like to be a Socialist.' To which Neish replied with savage dryness: 'Mebbe ye'd better j'st try it some time and see?' Oh dear, oh dear, thought Mrs. Miniver; from that moment on she resigned herself to a headache, and got it. Silly of Teresa. She herself, if Teresa had asked her to, could have battled with Agnes far more effectively, because from a closer range. But between a woman who thought that for her kitchenmaid to use face-powder was the beginning of Bolshevism, and a man who believed that the 30-mile speed limit was the thin end of the Totalitarian wedge, there could be no useful interchange of ideas.

Besides, Mrs. Miniver was beginning to feel more than a little weary of exchanging ideas (especially political ones) and of hearing other people exchange theirs. It's all very well, she reflected, when the ideas have had time to flower, or at least to bud, so that we can pick them judiciously, present them with a bow, and watch them unfold in the warmth of each other's understanding: but there is far too much nowadays of pulling up the wretched little things just to see how they are growing. Half the verbal sprigs we hand each other are nothing but up-ended rootlets, earthy and immature: left longer in the ground they might have come to something, but once they are exposed we seldom manage to replant them. It is largely the fault, no doubt, of the times we live in. Things happen too quickly, crisis follows crisis, the soil of our minds is perpetually disturbed. Each of us, to relieve his feelings, broadcasts his own running commentary on the preposterous and bewildering events of the hour: and this, nowadays, is what passes for conversation. For once in a way Mrs. Miniver felt glad when her hostess, with a scythe-like sweep of the eye, mowed down the women and carried them off (unprotesting Sabines) to the drawing-room. Agnes Lingfield, her very shoulder-blades expressing a sense of outrage, preceded the others up the stairs and retired at once, in rather marked silence, to powder her nose.

'Teresa, you are very naughty. How *could* you?'

'Put Neish next to Agnes? My dear, she's a joke woman; cross between a Wallis Mills and a Helen Hokinson. She's got fatty degeneration of the soul. Do her a lot of good to be shaken up.'

'Up to a point, yes. But not quite so violently as that. It's probably made her think that everybody who is even faintly progressive is like Neish. And it's certainly made *him* think that everybody who doesn't belong to the extreme Left is like Agnes. I shall have to spend the rest of the evening trying to convince him that they aren't.'

'Do, darling,' said Teresa impenitently. 'That'll be just your line. As a matter of fact,' she added, 'I very much doubt whether people like Neish and Agnes ever think at all. They just feel.'

'Oh, no,' said Mrs. Miniver. 'They do both, I'm certain. But the trouble is, they keep the two processes entirely separate. They've never learnt to think with their hearts or feel with their minds.'

'That sounds grand,' said Teresa ironically (they were old friends). 'Does it mean anything, or were you just trying it out to see what it sounded like?'

'It either means nothing at all,' said Mrs. Miniver, 'or else it's the discovery of the century. I'll think it over and let you know.'

Agnes Lingfield came back into the room, her face more nearly matt but her eyes still gleaming.

'Well, Teresa. I *must* say, your Left-wing friends . . .'

Oh, Lord, thought Mrs. Miniver, we're off again; and, anyway, I'm sick and tired of being offered nothing but that same old choice. Left wing . . . Right wing . . . it's so limited; why doesn't it ever occur to any of them that what one is really longing for is the wishbone?

'Doing a Mole'

Mrs. Miniver, having dropped the younger children at the seaside bungalow where they were going to stay with a school friend of Judy's, decided to spend an hour in the neighbouring town before driving back to London. It was to this town that she had been sent for a fortnight every year as a small child, and she felt a sudden desire to do a Mole. ('Doing a Mole' was Vin's phrase – coined after reading *The Wind in the Willows* – for a revisitation of old haunts.)

Having parked the car, she walked along the front in the fresh dancing sunlight. This part of the town was almost unrecognizable – a street of angular lettering and neon strips, with ice-cream tricycles instead of the old painted hokey-pokey barrows. As for the children's clothes – she tried to imagine what her old nurse would have said if she had wanted to walk from their lodgings to the beach in a wisp of a cotton sun-suit. She herself had worn no fewer than ten separate garments, including woollen combinations (folded thickly above the knee because they were too long) and baggy blue serge knickers into which all the rest of her clothes were tucked when she paddled, so that her shadow on the sand was always that of a gnome. Even in the sea she had worn blue serge, and on cold days a white Shetland spencer on top of her bathing-dress. She could still remember what it felt like when her nurse pulled it off over her wrists, wet.

At the pier she stopped and leant over the railings, hardly daring to draw a breath for fear of not finding what she was hoping for. She gave a cautious sniff, and then a luxurious one. It was all right. Evidently the most progressive of Town Councils could not do away with the peculiar, complex, deliciously nasty smell which is to be found under piers around high-water mark; a mixture of salt, rust, and slime, of rotting seaweed, dead limpets, and dried orange-peel. For a few moments, breathing it in, Mrs. Miniver could almost hear the creaking of her nurse's stays as she settled her broad back against the breakwater for the afternoon.

But presently the sight of a concert-party announcement brought her back again to the present day: for the name she read there was that of a sophisticated ensemble which she had often heard on the wireless. This was a far cry from the seaside entertainments of her childhood – the slightly shop-soiled-looking pierrots, and the sham nigger minstrels with straw hats, banjos, and bones.

It was one of these, curiously enough, who had first introduced her to death. He sang a song which began:—

What's (*plonk!*) the use (*plonk!*) of saving up your
     money,
If you can't take it with you when you die? (*plink-
     plonk!*)

and ended:—

But if (*plonk!*) you've got (*plonk!*) a wart upon your
     nose,
Well, you must take it with you when you die (*plink-
     plonk!*).

This, for some reason, pierced her to the heart with a shaft of realization. She burst into tears and flung herself across her nurse's grey tweed lap. 'I don't want to die!' she sobbed. 'Oh,

Nannie, I don't ever want to die!' The nurse, horrified, picked her up and carried her out of the pavilion. 'There, there,' she kept saying helplessly; 'there, there.' And that night she gave her a dose of magnesia.

Just beyond the pier Mrs. Miniver turned up a steep, curved street with a church in it. This was where their lodgings had been. She had no idea of the number, but she felt certain she would know the house when she came to it. Here again her nose had a good memory, for a breath of sickly-sweet scent brought her to a sudden standstill. Of course: she had quite forgotten about the privet hedge. And with that memory came another: there had been four panes of coloured glass in the middle of the front door – green, red, yellow, and blue. Looking through them in turn from the hall, you could make it be whatever season you liked in the front garden – spring, summer, autumn, or winter: but when you opened the door there was never anything but the hard white glare of July. She pushed the gate open and walked quietly up the path, to make sure whether those coloured panes were still there. They were: but as she bent down (she had once stood on tiptoe) to look at them, the door was opened by a woman with a shopping basket on her arm.

'Oh!' Mrs. Miniver tried to look self-possessed. 'I was just going to ring. I – I'm looking for rooms. But if you're going out, it doesn't matter a bit.'

'No trouble,' said the landlady. So Mrs. Miniver had to go through with it, peering into room after room. In the second floor front she paused and looked round very carefully.

'This is a nice one,' she said. 'So big and airy.' But she was thinking, How low, how small; how time contracts the rooms of one's childhood, drawing the walls inwards and the ceilings down. What with the shrinkage and the redecoration (for now, of course, it had a porridgy modern wallpaper with an orange frieze) she would not have known it was the same room, if it hadn't been for the fireplace. This, she was relieved to see, was untouched. There was the same ornate ironwork, the same rather bad imitation Dutch tiles; and the lowest tile on the left was still loose. By wiggling it gently, she had discovered, you could slip this tile right out and put it back again; and once, on their last day, she had dug a hole in the plaster behind it with her nurse's nail-scissors and hidden a new farthing, in order to have some buried treasure to look for the next time they came. But there had been no next time.

'I wonder,' she thought, eyeing the loose tile – but no, it was ridiculous, things didn't happen like that. Besides, one really couldn't . . .

'There now!' said the landlady. 'That's the bell. Excuse me a moment.'

Mrs. Miniver made a bee-line for the fireplace, knelt down and wiggled gently. Her heart was thumping: she knew now what burglars must go through. The tile came out quite easily: the hole was still there, but the farthing was gone. She slipped the tile back, stood up, and managed to get her knees dusted just before the landlady reached the top of the stairs.

Afterwards, walking down the steep street towards the beach, she thought about that farthing with an absurd and unreasonable pang. It would have made such a wonderful ending to her Mole. But she was comforted when she imagined with what incredulous delight some later child, exploring, must have found it.

The New Dimension

IT may or may not be true that conscience makes people cowardly: but it was certainly sea-sickness that made Mrs. Miniver brave, so far as air travel was concerned. Though you can hardly claim to be brave, she told herself ashamedly as she fastened the safety-strap across her knees, if your inside feels like curds and whey and your mouth is as dry as pumice. Resigned was a more suitable word for her state of mind. She had always had an exaggerated dread of the air: the reassuring statistics in the newspapers made no difference to her whatever. She was ready to admit that flying was safer than driving a car or crossing a crowded street; but she was irrationally convinced that if she herself went up in an aeroplane it was perfectly certain to crash. If it be not safe for me, she said in effect, what care I how safe it be? And so far neither the enthusiasm of her air-minded contemporaries, nor the calm assumption by the younger generation that it was the only possible way to travel, had ever been able to tempt her into the sky.

But, as every human being knows (for that term automatically excludes anybody who is 'a perfect sailor'), there are some sea journeys which can revolutionize all your feelings about death: and one of these is a crossing in bad weather from Kyle of Lochalsh to the Outer Isles. Mrs. Miniver had had the misfortune, ten days before, to coincide with a

summer gale: and, crawling weakly ashore at Lochmaddy, she
had sworn that nothing would induce her to cross the Little
Minch again, unless the weather changed.

The weather did change, of course. The wind dropped
suddenly. For more than a week the days were hot and still,
the water lapped gently, the narrow sickles of sand between
the headlands shone white in the sunlight and whiter under
the moon. The smaller islands looked like water-lily leaves
floating on a pool. The sea, all day, was blue; but at sunset it
was stained and streaked with rose, crimson, and purple, as
though some long-foundered ship with a cargo of wine had
suddenly broken open in its depths. But the evening before
she was due to leave, the wind rose as suddenly as it had
fallen. It blew and rained hard all night, and although by next
morning the sun was out again the sea was still heaving unat-
tractively. Mrs. Miniver took one look at it and wired to Sollas
Airport. It seemed to be the only thing to do; unless indeed
she was prepared to spend the rest of her life in the Hebrides,
nostalgically beholding in dreams the King's Road, Chelsea.

Peering out of the small rhomboidal window of the plane,
she wished, first, that some other passengers would come, to
give her confidence; and, second, that no other passengers
would come, so that her poltroonery might be unobserved.
For her face, she felt certain, must by now be noticeably green.

It seemed as though her second wish at any rate was going
to be granted, for there were only two minutes to go and she
was still alone. But at the last moment a ramshackle pony-cart
came down the road at full canter, and an enormous farmer,
followed by a young sheep-dog, clambered into the plane. He
turned at the door, shouted something in Gaelic to the woman
who drove the cart, and lowered himself gingerly into a seat
which seemed far too frail to hold him. The dog, with vast
unconcern, curled up on the floor and went to sleep.

'I thought I would be loossing the plane,' observed the
farmer pleasantly. 'It wass my watch that wass fall-ty.' He
tugged out an old silver turnip and adjusted it with care.

'Do you often fly?' asked Mrs. Miniver. He looked so marvellously incongruous.

'Oh – yess.' He seemed mildly surprised at the question. 'I have a brother in Barra. It iss very convenient.' His matter-of-factness was reassuring; and she needed reassurance badly, for the plane was now lumbering forward over the rough grass of the landing-field.

'This is my first flight,' she yelled above the noise of the engines. She felt rather desperately that she had to tell somebody. 'As a matter of fact, I'm scared stiff.' She smiled, to pretend she was exaggerating; but she knew that she wasn't. 'I suppose,' she added, 'I shan't mind so much when it's actually up.'

'But it *iss* up,' said the farmer. And sure enough, looking out of the window, she saw that the incredible had happened. They were in the air. She could see the rocky headlands edged with a white frill of foam; the deserted crofts, the dry-stone dykes, the green ridge-and-furrow of the lazy-beds whose only harvest nowadays was the wild iris; and, as they gained height, the whole extraordinary pattern of North Uist, so netted and fretted with lochs that it looked like a piece of lace.

Some hours later, in the train between Glasgow and Stirling, she tried to sort out her impressions. How hopelessly people fail, she thought, when they try to describe flying to someone who has never done it. They leave out all the really important things. They tell you that it saves time and (taking everything into account) money; they tell you that it makes the earth look like a map, cows like ants, and cars like beetles. But they don't tell you that it is staggering, tremendous; that it is not merely an experience but a re-birth; that it gives you for the first time in your life the freedom of a new dimension (for although we know that there are three of them, we are forced to move mainly in two: so that our sense of up-and-downness is necessarily dim and undeveloped compared with our acute perception of the to-and-fro). They

don't tell you that when you are up there it is the aeroplane
that seems to be the safe solid core of things, while the earth
is a distant planet upon which unfamiliar beings move among
unthinkable dangers. They don't tell you, either, that you will
be torn all the time between an immense arrogance and an
immense humility, so that you are at one moment God and at
the next a nameless sparrow. Nor do they tell you what it
feels like to thread your way among the noble and exciting
architecture of the clouds; nor how – best of all – you may
suddenly find a rainbow arched across the tip of your wing, as
though you had caught it in passing and carried it along with
you.

If only they had told her these things, she would have
flown long ago: for the promise of so much enchantment
would have overcome fear.

London in August

THE woman at the far end of the Park seat kept on nervously twisting and untwisting her handkerchief as though in acute mental distress. She was muttering to herself, too, under her breath. Mrs. Miniver glanced at her sideways once or twice, wondering what was wrong and wishing there was something she could do about it; but all of a sudden the woman, noticing her glances, looked up and smiled quite cheerfully.

'It's me First Aid,' she explained. 'I do get so muddled up with them knots. The lecturer, she says, "Right over left, left over right," see? But it never seems to come out the same, not when I do it meself.'

'I wonder,' suggested Mrs. Miniver tentatively, 'whether you'd find it any easier if you thought about it as "back and front"?'

The woman experimented with this idea for a few moments, and then her brow cleared as if by magic.

'Well, that's funny! So it is! It all depends on how you look at things, doesn't it?'

She laid the knotted handkerchief on the palm of her hand and beamed at it as proudly as though she had just made a successful cake. Oh, well, thought Mrs. Miniver; even if no other good comes out of the present condition of the world, at least there soon won't be a person left in England who doesn't know how to tie a reef-knot. And that's always something.

'I must say,' the other woman confided, 'I *do* enjoy me First Aid classes. It's like being back at school again – makes you feel quite young.'

'I know,' said Mrs. Miniver. Yes, she thought, that's the whole point. That is the one great compensation for the fantastic way in which the events of our time are forcing us to live. The structure of our life – based as it is on the ever-present contingency of war – is lamentably wrong: but its texture, oddly enough, is pleasant. There is a freshness about, a kind of rejuvenation: and this is largely because almost everybody you meet is busy learning something. Whereas in ordinary times the majority of grown-up people never try to acquire any new skill at all, either mental or physical: which is why they are apt to seem, and feel, so old.

She looked at her watch, got up, and walked on towards Kensington Gardens, where Clem had said he would meet her for tea if he could. His latest job was a big new school on Campden Hill which had to be finished early in September: this gave him a reason, and Mrs. Miniver an excellent excuse, for spending a good deal of August in London. The children were away, and so were the maids; Mrs. Burchett came in every morning to do their breakfast, and they had the rest of their meals out.

London in August, Mrs. Miniver had long ago discovered, is bleak in theory but enjoyable in practice. For one thing, your circle of acquaintances, without any of the pangs of bereavement or estrangement, is arbitrarily reduced to half its normal size, with some interesting results. You find yourself knowing better, quite suddenly, people with whom you have been at a standstill for years; understudies blossom into stars; even toads occasionally reveal an unsuspected jewel in the head. And the town itself, too, has a strange charm, in spite of the shuttered houses, the empty window-boxes, the dusty plane-trees, and the smell of hot asphalt. Or perhaps, in a

way, because of these. For young Johnny Flint (whose poems,
she noticed, had lately been getting more personal and less
political) had said yesterday that anybody who had a genuine
passion for London got a particular pleasure out of being
there at this time of year, 'as you do out of being with somebody you're really in love with when they're looking very
tired and rather plain.' So *that* was it. Thank goodness, Mrs.
Miniver had thought, as she always did when any of her
friends came into love or money. She wondered idly who it
could be, but knew that with poets this didn't really matter.
Beatrice, Fanny Brawne, Ann More, the Dark Lady of the
Sonnets – they are all one and the same person: or perhaps no
person at all. Happy or unhappy, kind or unkind, they are
nothing but bundles of firewood.

> And it will matter little, in after days,
> Whether this twig, or that, kindled the blaze.

It was four o'clock. This was the hour when at any other
time of year the great tide of perambulators, which is drawn
up into the Park twice a day by some invisible and unvarying
moon, would have been on the ebb. They would have been
streaming steadily out through every gateway, back to the
nursery tea-tables of Bayswater, Kensington, Brompton,
Belgravia and Mayfair: sleek, shining, graceful, expensive
perambulators, well-built, well-sprung, well-upholstered,
pushed by well-trained nurses and occupied by well-bred,
well-fed children. What that woman at the luncheon-party
had called Really Nice Children: the sort of children who
had rocking-horses, and special furniture with rabbits on it,
and hats and coats that matched, and grandmothers with
houses in the country. But in August the shores of the Park
were forsaken by this tide, and another one took its place.
They straggled over the worn, slippery grass in little proces-
sions – whey-faced, thin, ragged, merry and shrewd. The
boys carried nets and jam-jars. The eldest girl, almost always,

was lugging a dilapidated push-chair with an indeterminate
baby in it; and sometimes an ex-baby as well, jammy-
mouthed and lolling over the edge.

These were the other children. With any luck, if there was
a war before they grew up, they would one day see cows, and
running streams, and growing corn. But not otherwise.
Unless, of course, a miracle happened; unless the structure
could be changed without altering the texture, and the people
of England, even after the necessity for it had been averted,
remembered how to tie a reef-knot.

Back from Abroad

'*PARTIR, c'est mourir un peu. . . .*' How shrewdly the
French language can drive home a nail, thought Mrs.
Miniver, seeing again in her mind's eye the row of smiling
faces to which she had waved a regretful good-bye, the
evening before, from the window of the little Alpine train. At
her sister-in-law's request she had travelled out with her niece
Alison, who was going to spend six months living with a
Swiss family; and she had stayed on for a week at a *pension* in
the same village, just to see that Alison was happily established. The whole family had come to see her off at the
station. The solitary porter, standing beside his yellow toy
barrow, had had a grass stalk between his teeth; and the
moon, just topping the Mittelhorn, had looked for the space
of a breath or two like a vast snow-ball which was about to
roll down the glacier.

But why, she wondered, as the serene but unjoyful landscape
of northern France slid past the dining-car windows – the
white horses, the dun cattle, the red farms, the grey shutters,
the beaded cemeteries, the hedgeless fields like foreheads without eyebrows – why has nobody ever made the parallel
observation: '*Revenir, c'est savoir ce que c'est que d'être un
revenant*'? That would be no less shrewd: for when you first
come home from a strange place you are always something of a
ghost. They were sorry when you went away, and they welcome

you back with affection: but in the meanwhile they have adjusted their lives a little to your absence. For the first meal or two, there is not quite enough room for your chair. They ask, 'Where did you go? What was it like?'; but for the life of you you cannot tell them. You can say, 'It was like a large, neat Scotland'; or 'They use *nonante* instead of *quatre-vingt-dix*'; or, 'They trim all their buildings with wooden lace'; or, 'There was a nice little German boy staying at the *pension*'; or 'I made friends with a charming farmer at the village fête.' But however eagerly they listen they do not really take in what you are saying. For you cannot make them understand the essential point, which is that when you went away you took the centre of the universe with you, so that the whole thing went on revolving, just as usual, round your own head. How could they, indeed, be expected to believe this, when they know quite well that all the time the centre of everything stayed at home with them? It is a day or two, as a rule, before your universe and theirs (like the two images in a photo-graphic range-finder) merge and become concentric: and when that happens, you know you are really home.

But that moment, for Mrs. Miniver, was still far ahead. She had not even quite detached herself yet from the place she had just left. Like the earth-bound spirit of one who has recently died, she still thought in terms of the life she had been leading. Glancing up at the clock of the dining-car, she reflected: 'Hansi's mother will just be tying the napkin round his neck; and he will be saying "*Bit*-te, Mama, *keinen Blumenkohl.*"' The first time she had heard him say this she had caught his mother's eye and smiled: for the tone and the sentiment were so exactly Toby's. She had smiled, too, when she overheard at breakfast the so familiar question: '*Aber du, Hansi, hast du dir die Zähne gut geputzt?*' But she had done more than smile when Hansi, after a day or two's distant politeness, had taken her by the hand and led her to a row of curiously-shaped pebbles in a secret hiding-place between the wood-stacks.

'*Meine Sammlung*,' he said briefly. 'My c'lection,' echoed
Toby's voice in her memory. Her heart turned over: how
could there be this ridiculous talk of war, when little boys in
all countries collected stones, dodged cleaning their teeth,
and hated cauliflower?

Indeed, what always struck her when she went abroad
was how much stronger the links are between people of the
same calling than between people of the same race: especially if it is a calling which has more truck with the laws of
nature than with the laws of man. The children of the world
are one nation; the very old, another; the blind, a third: (for
childhood, age and blindness are all callings, and hard ones
at that). A man who works with wood, a man who works
with iron, a man who works with test-tubes, is more akin to
a joiner, a smith, a research chemist from the other end of
the earth than to a clerk or a shopkeeper in his own town. A
fisherman from Ushant and a fisherman from Stornoway
are both citizens of the same relentless country; and
Nicollier, the farmer with whom Mrs. Miniver had made
friends at the village fête, had expressed in a different tongue
precisely the same feelings and opinion as Tom (Brickwall)
Iggulsden.

If only, she thought, sipping her black coffee, one could
somehow get them together – not the statesmen and the
diplomats, but Toby and Hansi, Iggulsden and Nicollier. If
only all governments would spend the price of a few bombers
on exchanging for the holidays, free of charge, a certain
number of families from each district. . . .

The attendant brought her bill. She paid it, burying her
last thought as a dog buries a bone, to be returned to later.
They had passed Boulogne now and were on the last lap of
the journey to Calais. As one does when there are only a few
minutes to go and it is not worth while embarking on anything new, she let her gaze wander round the carriage, idly
seeking the titillation of the printed word. On the window-sill
she read:—

Ne pas se pencher en dehors.
Nicht hinauslehnen.
E pericoloso sporgersi.

Exactly, she thought. 'What I tell you three times is true.'
But the trouble was, it still had to be said in three different
languages. . . .

At the Hop-Picking

Brickwall Farm consisted mostly of fruit and pasture: so few acres were under hops that Tom Iggulsden did not engage any professional pickers from London. He did the picking himself, with the aid of his wife, his mother, his five children, and any of the neighbours who cared to lend a hand: which generally included the whole Miniver family.

This time the Minivers were enjoying it even more than usual. Before, they had always been mere casual helpers, doing it for fun and leaving off whenever they felt inclined. But this year they knew that Tom Iggulsden was really counting on them, for he was short of his three best workers. Both his sons had been called up, and his eldest daughter Ivy had gone off to try and get a job in a munition factory.

Old Mrs. Iggulsden, who was picking into the same bin as Mrs. Miniver, disapproved of Ivy's behaviour and was saying so with some force.

'She never 'ad naow sanse, diddn' Ive. Gooin' arf jus' 'fore de 'aapin', an' leavin' 'er Dad short'anded. . . . Reckon I'd 've prin'nigh flawed 'er alive, if I'd 'a' bin Taam.'

'Now den, Ma,' said Tom Iggulsden with a grin, stretching up his long-poled knife to cut down a bine. He laid the thick twisted swag of greenery across the canvas bin and winked at Mrs. Miniver behind his mother's back.

'You git aan wid y'r owan jaab, Ma, an' leave Ivy be. If she rackoned she ought to goo, she 'ad to goo, diddn' she?'

'I don' see naow sort o' sanse in it,' mumbled the old woman, quite unconvinced. "She'd be doin' more good a-pickin' o' dese 'ere 'aaps fer to goo into folk's bellies, dan a'makin' o' dem old bullets fer to goo into deir 'eads.'

Tom Iggulsden's wife, overhearing this from the next bin, shot an apologetic glance at Mrs. Miniver. She had a light hand with pastry but was a little inclined to be genteel; and her mother-in-law's robustness of speech often made her uncomfortable, especially in front of 'foreigners.'

'Of course,' put in Mrs. Miniver diplomatically, 'some people would try to make out that hops were nearly as bad as bullets. Teetotallers, I mean.'

'Oh – *dem!*' said old Mrs. Iggulsden with royal scorn. She stripped off her next handful of cones almost vindictively: they fell into the half-full bin without a sound, light, soft and ghostly, a dozen little severed heads of teetotallers.

Presently there came the familiar cry of the bin-man, who walked round every so often to ladle the hops out into ten-bushel pokes.

'*Git* your 'aaps ready, please!'

Warned of his approach, they left off picking and set to work to clear out all the odd leaves and pieces of stalk which had dropped in by mistake. This was the part that the children enjoyed most, because it meant leaning right over the edge and plunging one's arms elbow-deep into the feathery goldy-green mass.

The role of bin-man, this year, was played by Tom Iggulsden himself, in the intervals of cutting down bines; and his assistant, who held the mouth of the poke open, was Vin. When the two of them arrived everybody stopped working and tried to guess how many measures there would be in the bin.

'Twalve, I rackon,' said old Mrs. Iggulsden.

'Fifteen,' said Judy hopefully. But Tom, taking the first scoop with his wicker basket, said 'Thirteen.' And thirteen it turned out to be.

It was certainly a relief to knock off for a bit, to straighten one's back and stretch out one's fingers. They had been going hard at it ever since lunch-time, with the effortless industry which is born of working with good company, in pleasant surroundings, at a perceptibly progressing task. It was like knitting: you couldn't bear to stop until you had done one more row, one more bine. But it was also like watching the sea come in on a calm day, as the soft green tide crept steadily up the brown cliffs of the bin.

Old Mrs. Iggulsden reached under her stool for a bottle and took a generous swig.

'*Ma* . . .!' said her daughter-in-law, going through hell.

"'Aaps outside needs 'aaps inside,' said the old woman cheerfully. 'Ain't that right, Mrs. Mimver?' She wiped her mouth on the back of her hand. Her briar-root fingers, which could still strip a bine more quickly than most people's, were stained black with juice and covered with scratches from the rough clinging stems. So indeed were everybody's, except for those who were not too proud to wear gloves. But though gloves could protect one from stains and scratches, nothing could protect one from the drowsiness, the nearly irresistible drowsiness, which comes over all but the most hardened towards the end of a long day's picking. It seems to be more than a scent that emanates from the hops: it is almost a visible miasma, sweet yet agreeably acrid, soothing yet tonic, which blurs the edges of one's thoughts with a greenish-gold glow.

'Where's Toby?' said Mrs. Miniver suddenly. Nobody knew.

'I 'a'n't seen nothin' of 'im since dinner-time,' said Mrs. Iggulsden. 'Ver' like 'e'll be down at the fur bin along o' Molly.'

But he was not at the far bin, nor at any of the others. Mrs. Miniver, always a little uneasy about the main road, went off to look for him. It was extraordinary how soon, wandering through the narrow leafy aisles, one got out of sight of the others. For a short time their voices followed her: the broad vowels, the clipped consonants, the unvarying parabolas of the Kentish speech. But from a few rows further on she could neither see nor hear them. She was alone in the heart of a silent, orderly jungle; a jungle which was like one of the most advanced patterns in a gigantic game of cat's cradle. Wherever she stopped to call or listen for Toby, she found herself at the converging point of eight green alleys; and from the root of every plant four strings stretched upwards and outwards to the wire trellis overhead, each with two bines climbing round it the way of the sun. (And why, in the name of an inscrutable providence, should hops always twine with the sun, while scarlet runners invariably went a-widdershin?)

Getting no answer to her cries, she walked back towards the pickers. And there, just out of sight of the last bin, lay Toby, fast asleep on a pile of pokes, with a leafy bine trailing right across him: a small rosy Bacchus with juice-stained hands. She smiled, and covered him up with an empty sack. There was no need to wake him until it was time to go home.

'From Needing Danger . . .'

Dearest Susan,

Thank you for your long letter. I began one to you the day
before war broke out, but until this evening I haven't had
time to sit down and finish it. And when I re-read it just now
it was like reading a letter by a different person, so much has
one's mood changed in the last few weeks. So I tore it up.

You say, tell you facts and feelings. Well, facts first, they're
easier. Clem's A.A. Battery is quartered in a girls' school,
from which he writes superbly funny letters. The girls are
absent, of course, but their school-stories are there, and he is
finding these a fascinating study. His favourite chapter-heading, so far, is 'Monica Turns Out a Decent Sort'; but at
present he is absorbed in a last-war one about a games mis-
tress who was a spy in disguise and used to write code
messages on tennis-balls and throw them into the North Sea.
He says he can hardly wait to get to the end. He is also
making a collection of *graffiti*, which are all quite touchingly
mild. Things like 'Gwenny T. is a Big Pig' and 'Molly B. is a
Brat.' There is a very dignified one, which simply says: 'I
think Gwenny T. is the most hateful person I have ever met.'
And another, arranged like an equation: 'Violet W.+Gwenny

T.=Lovey-dovey. ∴ Ha! ha!' Clem says he was so relieved to find that *somebody* liked poor Gwenny T. after all.

The children are down here, having the time of their lives with our seven tough and charming evacuees – but I'll tell you more about that next time I write. Mrs. Downce has played up admirably. I was rather afraid she might be pot-faced, but not a bit of it. To tell you the truth I think she is delighted to have some Cockney voices in the house. It makes her feel at home after her twenty-five years in Darkest Kent. She had quite a Dr.-Livingstone-I-presume expression on her face when she welcomed them in.

Ellen (our present incarnation of the cosmic principle of house-parlourmaid, successor to Gladys, who got married) is down here, too, helping Nannie and Mrs. D. Mrs. Adie is in London, sleeping in the kitchen so as not to have to traipse downstairs when the raid-warning goes. 'Well, Madam,' she said with a wry smile, 'I never thought I'd live to be glad that I couldna persuade ye to shift into one o' yon new non-basements. The Lord,' she added solemnly, 'doesna seem to care how much trouble He gies Himself in order to bring us to our senses.' I was amused at the time, and sent Clem an elaborate picture in coloured chalk of guns, tanks, and aeroplanes charging across Europe, with a Jovial bearded face directing operations from a cloud in the left-hand top corner, and a repentant Mrs. Adie in the right-hand bottom one. But during the last fortnight I've begun to feel – N.B., we are now on to feelings – that she may be right, after all. As you know, she has a real Scots genius for coining phrases, and it is extraordinary how often they ring true.

The thing is, we're all so buoyed up just now with the crusading spirit, and so burningly convinced of the infamy of the Government we're fighting against (this time, thank goodness, one doesn't say 'the nation we're fighting against') – that we're a little inclined to forget about our own past idiocies. The fact that we are now crusaders needn't blind us to the fact that for a very long time we have been, as

Badger would say, echidnas. I can think of a hundred ways already in which the war has 'brought us to our senses.' But it oughtn't to *need* a war to make a nation paint its kerb-stones white, carry rear-lamps on its bicycles, and give all its slum children a holiday in the country. And it oughtn't to need a war to make us talk to each other in buses, and invent our own amusements in the evenings, and live simply, and eat sparingly, and recover the use of our legs, and get up early enough to see the sun rise. However, it *has* needed one: which is about the severest criticism our civilization could have.

I wonder whether it's too much to hope that afterwards, when all the horrors are over, we shall be able to conjure up again the feelings of these first few weeks, and somehow rebuild our peace-time world so as to preserve everything of war which is worth preserving? What we need is a kind of non-material war museum, where, instead of gaping at an obsolete uniform in a glass case, we can press a magic button and see a vision of ourselves as we were while this revealing mood was freshly upon us. I know that this sounds silly and that there are no such magic buttons. The nearest approach to them, I think, are the poems and articles – and even the letters and chance phrases – which are struck out of people like sparks at such moments as this. So write all the letters you can, Susan, please (to me, if you feel like it, but at any rate to somebody), and keep all the ones you get, and put down somewhere, too, everything you see or hear which will help later on to recapture the spirit of this tragic, marvellous, and eye-opening time: so that, having recaptured it, we can use it for better ends. We may not, of course, ever get the chance: but if we do, and once more fail to act upon it, I feel pretty sure we shan't be given another one.

As usual in all moments of stress, I've been falling back on Donne. It's a pity preachers never seem to take their texts from anything but the Bible: otherwise they could base a perfectly terrific sermon for the present day on verse 16 of his

Litany – the one which begins 'From needing danger . . .' Do look it up – I know there's a copy in the library at Quern, in the little bookshelf just on the left of the fireplace.

Yours ever, with much love,

Caroline.

Mrs. Miniver Makes a List

'WILL ye be wanting anything more tonight, mem?' asked Mrs. Adie, putting the coffee down by the fire and picking up Mrs. Miniver's supper-tray.

'No, thank you, nothing at all. As soon as I've made out my list of Christmas presents, I'm going straight to bed.'

Mrs. Adie paused at the door, tray in hand.

'Ay,' she said. 'This is going to be a queer kind of Christmas for the bairns, with their Daddy away.'

'I dare say he'll get leave,' said Mrs. Miniver hopefully.

'Mebbe ay, mebbe no.' Mrs. Adie was not one to encourage wishful thinking. 'To say nothing,' she added, 'of having ten bairns in the house, instead of three. My! It'll take me back to when I was a wean myself.'

'Why, there weren't ten of you, were there?'

'Thirteen,' said Mrs. Adie, wearing the particular expression that Clem always called 'Scotland Wins.'

Mrs. Miniver was surprised, not so much by the information itself as by the fact that Mrs. Adie had vouchsafed it. She was not in the habit of talking about her own childhood. Indeed, she rather gave the impression that she had never had one, but had simply risen from the foam, probably somewhere just off the East Neuk of Fife.

'Well, I'll say good night, mem.'

'Good night, Mrs. Adie. That was a lovely Welsh rabbit.'

Left alone, Mrs. Miniver poured out a cup of coffee and sat on the fender-stool to drink it, roasting her back. Yes, it was going to be a queer Christmas for everybody this year. To the parents left behind in the big cities it would seem only half a Christmas; to the hard-pressed foster-parents in the country, a double one. Out of her own seven evacuees at Starlings, only two, she knew, had ever had a tree of their own. And Reen, the eldest – a shrill, wizened, masterful little creature of twelve, who in the last two months had become so touchingly less shrill and wizened (though no less masterful) – had never even hung up her stocking. She was inclined to scoff at the idea of taking to this custom so late in life.

'Ony kids do that,' she said. 'It's sissy.'

'Vin still does it,' said Mrs. Miniver. 'He's nearly sixteen, and he's not in the least sissy.'

'Are you sure?' asked Reen suspiciously.

'Quite sure,' said Mrs. Miniver, without a twitch. (She must tell Vin this, next time she wrote.)

But it was too early yet to make plans about stockings. First of all, she must get on with that list of presents. She put down her coffee-cup and went resolutely over to the writing-table.

One of Mrs. Miniver's bad habits – which, like many bad habits, was only an exaggeration of a good one – was that she was apt to begin by being methodical and to end by being a magpie. It was, for instance, quite a sound idea to keep one's Christmas present list until the following year, so as to make sure that one didn't leave people out or give them the same thing twice running. But the worst of it was, she never could bring herself to throw away the old lists when they were done with; and as she had started the habit when she first married, she had now accumulated no less than seventeen of them. Not only did they take up an unnecessary amount of space in an already overcrowded drawer, but they caused her to waste time at a season of the year when time was most valuable: for whenever she opened the drawer to consult last year's list, she found herself quite unable to resist browsing through the earlier ones.

For the last eight years the opening names had not varied at all: *Clem, Vin, Judy, Toby, Nannie, Mrs. Adie, Mrs. Downce, Downce.* The ninth name had changed, at intervals of about two years, from Norah to Jessie, from Jessie to Gladys, and from Gladys to Ellen: for there seemed to be something fatally marriageable, as well as incurably trochaic, about the Minivers' house-parlourmaids. Even Ellen, as unglamorous a girl as you could wish to meet, who had come to them a few months ago completely heart-whole, had already acquired a young man. Clem, to whom Mrs. Miniver had broken this news in a letter, had written back saying, 'For heaven's sake, next time, go for a dactyl or a monosyllable. They may have less S.A.'

As the lists went farther back, however, important gaps appeared. Nine years ago there had been no Toby; twelve years ago, no Judy. Yet at each of these Christmases, she remembered, her universe (which would now be unthinkable without them) had seemed complete. As for Vin, he figured in all the lists except the first two; and as she traced his presents backwards from last year's spinning-rod through conjuring sets and Red Indian outfits to the woolly rabbit of fifteen years ago, she felt that she was seeing the whole story of his childhood in reverse, like one of those trick films where the spilt milk pours itself back into the jug.

She laid down the sheets on top of each other, one by one. Vin grew up again before her mind's eye: became three, four, in a sun-suit and a floppy linen hat; became seven, eight, in grey flannel shorts (so like, and yet so unlike, Toby); became twelve, thirteen, in long trousers; shot upwards past her elbow, her shoulder, her head; and finally grinned down at her from six inches above it (so like, and yet so unlike, Clem).

Parallel with this memory-film ran another, whose only visible track was the column of prices on the right-hand side of the page. Amplified by her recollection, these scribbled figures made a pretty accurate record of the Miniver family's material ups and downs. There was the lavishness of the first two years, based on youthful ignorance, a fixed salary, and a regular parental allowance; there were the soberer standards which became necessary when Clem started out on his own; there were the deceptive early successes, the too optimistic move to a larger house. Then the slump, the difficult years; the years when an acute appendicitis seemed to take a malevolent pleasure in coinciding with an ultimatum from the bank; when they tossed on the horns of the professional classes' eternal dilemma – whether to retrench openly, or to bluff things out for the sake of keeping up appearances in front of potential clients. The years when, after dining out, they said No, thanks, they'd rather walk and pick up a taxi, it would be so nice to get a breath of air; and when their Christmas presents to each other (since they couldn't cut down too drastically on anybody else's) dwindled by mutual consent into mere tokens, which they exchanged in front of the children with elaborate ceremony, delighted exclamations, and a great deal of coloured wrapping-paper. Not that they needed tokens; but it would have shocked the children if they had exchanged nothing at all.

Things had looked up again, eventually. Clem built an unusual country house for Sandro Baltman, and Sandro talked, and that set the ball rolling fast. By the time Toby was born they had been able to buy Starlings and to get the Downces to look after it. The tokens had expanded into proper presents again, and ever since then the total at the bottom of the right-hand column had been getting a little larger every year. But both of them, fortunately, had good memories: and when young married couples came to dine with them, they always said, 'Yes, of course; you're sure to find one on the rank just round the corner.'

Mrs. Miniver put the last sheet back on top of the others and clipped them all together again. No, she could not possibly throw them away: they contained too much of her life.

Besides, however clear one's memories seemed to be, it did one no harm to polish them up from time to time. One is what one remembers: no more, no less.

She took a clean sheet of paper and wrote across the top in neat block capitals:

'CHRISTMAS 1939'

Letters from Mrs. Miniver to The Times

Autumn 1939

Peace-In-War

Dearest Susan,

I have come back here to find a job, as Starlings now seems to be running perfectly all right, nursery, evacuees, and all. I don't know yet what kind of job I can get, if any. Driving, for choice. What I hanker for, of course, is to be put at the beck and call of some very important hush-hush sort of man who needs to be driven very fast in a long-nosed powerful car to mysterious destinations. From time to time my passenger would glance down at his watch, then backwards over his shoulder, and say briefly, 'Step on it, Mrs. M.' And I should see in the driving-mirror a supercharged straight eight, disguised as a grocer's van, rapidly gaining on us. . . . Yes, definitely, that would be just my cup of tea. But either this type of man is dying out – which I should deplore – or else, which is more likely, he does his own driving.

In the meanwhile I am helping at whatever odd jobs I can find – addressing envelopes, rolling bandages, &c. – and enjoying, more than I can say, being back in London, which is unbelievably impressive.

The funny thing is that although the floodlighting experiments used to reveal a whole lot of architectural beauties which one didn't know, the black-out reveals even more. One loses the details of buildings, but sees their outlines properly for the first time. That is, when there's any vestige of a moon. And even when there isn't, one still discovers new things by hearing, touch, and smell. For instance, I had never noticed before that the area railings in this Square were of such a pleasing design. Now I know them intimately, by touch. And I can tell when I'm getting near to the Air Raid Shelter at the corner by the damp jutey smell of the sandbags. In fact, the whole of London now smells most pleasantly of jute – even indoors, because of the stuff one uses for under-curtains. It is one of the best scents in the world: partly, I suppose, because it reminds one of those rickety tents one made out of sacking as a child.

As for the balloons – you've probably read a lot about them in the papers already, but I can't help that, I have got to talk about them. They are the most delightful and comforting companions in the world. You see, I hadn't been in London at all since war broke out, and when I travelled up five days ago, by the late train, I don't mind admitting I was feeling rather jittery. There was a serene gold sunset, with oast-houses sticking up against it like black cats, and all the way up in the train that wretched lovely line from *Antony and Cleopatra* kept running in my head:—

> Finish, good lady; the bright day is done,
> And we are for the dark.

I went to bed very sore about the shins from falling over a station barrow, and hating the house with neither Clem nor the children in it, and with Mrs. A. looking more than ever like John Knox; and altogether everything was rather grim. But when I looked out of my window early next morning and saw all those fat little silver watch-fish floating overhead in a clear sky, I felt completely reassured. They really are quite beautiful, although – like puppies – they manage to combine

this with being intrinsically comic. From time to time they
are taken down: ostensibly to refill them with gas, but really,
I suspect, to scrape off the barnacles. I only wish, once
they've got them down, they'd paint faces on them like
Chinese dragons. I'm sure it would add to their deterrent
effect. The best thing of all, which nobody had prepared me
for, is that on windy nights they *sing*. It's like going to sleep
on a ship at anchor, with the sound of wind in the rigging.
Only, thank goodness, London doesn't rock – yet.

There, I have finished letting off steam about the balloons.
Liberavi animam meam, as Uncle John always used to say
when he had just been particularly offensive to poor Aunt
Sarah. Like many well-read but ill-tempered people, he
thought a Latin tag excused everything. But Aunt Sarah
didn't know any Latin. Bad Luck.

As for other things, all I can say is that Hitler, poor mis-
guided man, has made the biggest mistake of his life in giving
us a month of this kind of peace-in-war in which to become
calm, collected, and what's more, *chic*. Of course, the people
who are natural born dowds still manage to make their gas
masks look dowdy, but those who are normally well-turned-
out somehow contrive to make them into a positive
decoration. It isn't only a question of having one of the many
expensive and pansified cases which are on the market,
though I admit they help: it's more that most people have
now learned to carry the things with an air – with *panache*.
You might think, walking about London, that everybody was
going off to a picnic with a box of special food.

Another thing: you know how in normal times, when they
come back to London in the autumn, English women make no
attempt to keep on wearing light, bright colours. They just
mutter 'Fogs' in a defeatist manner, put away their summer
handbags, gloves, scarves, and so forth, and then throw up
their arms and drown in a sea of black, navy, dark brown,
bottle, and maroon, as the fashion catalogues would say. This
year, wearing white 'accessories' has become literally a matter

of life and death – or at any rate, of wholeness and injury; and you've no idea how much more cheerful the place looks. But it's odd, isn't it, that the aim of 'protective colouring' should now be to detach us from our background, not to melt us into it? This war will have to introduce a new word for that process, just as the last one introduced 'camouflage.'

Talking of stockings, I remember Teresa saying last year that one of the most awful minor catastrophes in the world was when one's suspender gave way at a party: how one felt quite discomfited, and lop-sided, and altogether at a loss until it was done up again. Well, I think that's the main difference between September, 1938, and now. Then, we felt only too distinctly the uncomfortable *ping!* of the elastic. But now we've had time to do it up again, and we feel more than equal to coping with the party, however long and strenuous it may be.

How silly it was of him to allow us to become not only angry but bored. This nation is never really dangerous until it's bored.

Yours ever, with much love,

Caroline.

A Moonless Week

London
12th October 1939

Dearest Susan,

I now realize that when I wrote about the black-out in my last letter I was talking about something I hadn't seen. Last week, even before moonrise, there was always a faint glow. This week there is no moon at all, and it is really inky.

I haven't dined out far afield. During moonless weeks, I can see, the tendency is to behave as though one was living in the country without a car, and confine oneself to neighbours who are within groping distance. In fact, London is beginning to feel more and more like a country town, what with the tinkle of bicycle bells and the clopping of hoofs, both of which seem to become commoner every day. In the evening there is so little traffic that people's footsteps on the pavements make quite a loud clatter: before, one could hardly hear them. And apropos (literally for once) *des bottes*, you've no idea how all this walking has improved people's figures. Men with incipient pots, women who were developing Dunlop ridges above the belt, are now sylphlike. As for Clive Pritchard, he bicycles to his office every day and has become quite unpompous. There seems to be something about bicycling which induces humility; I suppose it's the slightly bowed attitude one has to adopt.

Another noticeable thing is the way people are taking advantage of the wide sandbag ledges to sit comfortably in the sun and eat their lunch. Up till now, we've never been allowed to have café tables out of doors 'because they would obstruct the pavements.' But now the pavements have been obstructed willy-nilly; and once English people have discovered the fun of eating in the fresh air and watching the passers-by, it's most unlikely that they'll ever again allow themselves to be cooped up indoors against their will.

Two things one misses, the first a little, the second badly. The first is golden windows. It used to be so lovely, that hour after the lamps were lit and before the curtains were drawn, when you could catch glimpses into other people's lives as you walked along the street: a kitchen table with a red bobbey cloth and a fat cook writing a letter, laboriously; or a ground-floor sitting-room, very spick and span, full of obvious wedding presents, with a brand new wife, rather touching and self-important, sitting sewing, her ears visibly tuned for the sound of a latch-key; or an old man by the fire, doing a cross-word, with an empty afternoon behind him and an empty evening in front. And occasionally, by great luck, a dining-room with a child's birthday party going on; a ring of lighted candles round the cake and a ring of lighted faces round the table; one face brighter than all the others, like a jewel on the ring. But now all this is gone. Houses slip straight from day to night, with tropical suddenness. There are no more glimpses; one can only guess.

The other thing I miss, terribly, is children. Not only my own – I do at least see them (and plenty of others) at week-ends: but children in general, as an ingredient of the town's population, a sort of leaven. It may be different in some parts of London, but certainly round here they have acquired a rarity interest. They used to be daisies and are now bee-orchises. One looks round with a lift of pleasure on hearing a child's voice in a bus, and can't take one's eyes off it the whole way, especially if it is young enough to talk and move inconsequently. But when one sees the gas-mask on its lap one's delight is tempered.

I went on Tuesday to the first of the National Gallery war-time concerts. An amazing experience. All sorts of people, young and old, smart and shabby, in uniform and out of it, soldiers, nurses, Salvation Army girls, typists, office-boys, old ladies with ear-trumpets, and a few of the regular 'musicals' with coiled plaits. All packed together, sitting on gilt chairs, on black chairs, on green canvas camp-chairs, on the white and brawn-coloured marble floor, even on the piano-dais itself; many others standing up, or leaning against the gilt frames where the big altar-pieces used to be. A few, perhaps, there out of curiosity, but most of them because they were suffering from a raging thirst for music, for tran-quillity re-collected through emotion, and for some assurance of pattern and order in a jangled world. She played magnifi-cently and thoughtfully, almost as though she were discovering – no, *un*covering – the music for the first time. Bach, Beethoven, Schubert, Brahms – ironical, isn't it, how the world has to turn to the great Germans to find healing for the spiritual wounds inflicted on it by the ignoble ones? There were so many people in tears that it might have been a revivalist meeting. So it was, in a way. And the curious thing was that everything she played seemed to have a kind of double loveliness, as though she had managed to distil into it all the beauty of the pictures that were missing from the walls. It was quite unforgettable.

With love, yours ever,

Caroline.

Some Points of View

Dearest Susan,

I've been collecting one or two opinions about the war, which you might like to hear. I don't mean about policy, and strategy, and what happened last week, and what's going to happen next; but about more personal (and therefore more universal, and therefore more important) aspects of it.

First of all, there's old Lady J., who has insisted on staying in London in spite of her daughter's efforts to get her down to Shropshire. 'Herbert thinks it's very immoral of me to stay here,' she said yesterday. (Herbert is her awful son-in-law.) 'He says, with his usual brutal frankness, that I shall be such a nuisance as an air-raid casualty. But you see, the chances are strongly against my being an air-raid casualty. I don't go out much, and I have had the library made into an excellent gas-proof shelter. Whereas if I go and live with Herbert and Dorothy I am absolutely certain to be a nuisance, day in, day out. I don't like the country – though I admit it's produced some capital poems – and I can't stand Herbert; and as for Dorothy, she's a dear good girl, but so dreadfully county. I did my best with her, and at one time I had hopes that she might marry somebody *quite* unsuitable. But she took after her father, and reverted to type.'

She's perfectly right, of course. In the country she would do nothing but sit over the fire, and seethe at Herbert, and look at poor Dorothy rather as a retired smuggler might look at a daughter who had married an Excise Officer. Whereas in London she's a godsend to all her friends. She keeps open house, and provides (among other meals) the most lovely breakfast parties for people who've just come off night duty. She does the cooking herself on a chafing-dish, wearing an elegant red velvet tea-gown, in that long panelled dining-room looking on to the garden. 'At my age,' she says, 'one wakes up abominably early anyhow, so one might as well get up and do something useful.' She also remarked the other day that the great thing about war was that it abolished old age. I said, rather densely, did she mean that people simply didn't live to be old? She said No, of course not: she meant that if you had already had the misfortune to get old you didn't feel so conscious of it in war-time, because then – in a modern war, at any rate – your expectation of life suddenly became very little shorter than anybody else's.

'It never occurred to me,' I said, surprised, 'that you worried about being old.' 'I don't as a rule,' she admitted. 'Only now and then, when I realize with a horrid shock that the person I am talking to is making allowances for me. I will not be made allowances for. Especially,' she added with a glint, 'by Herbert.'

What a contrast to Agnes Lingfield, whom I ran into in Sloane Street a few days ago. She insisted on taking me into a shop for a cup of coffee, and then sat with both elbows on the table, disseminating gloom. 'I haven't seen you since the day we lunched at Teresa's and she put me next to that terrible little Bolshie, what's-his-name.'

'Neish,' I said.

'Of course – Nash.'

'Neish,' I said.

'Leish. Oh well . . .' (One of my favourite studies is the way people like Agnes always mispronounce the names of anybody they dislike, especially if he or she is out of a lower drawer. It is such a pathetically naive weapon.)

'Anyway,' she went on – though I really couldn't see that it was relevant – 'look what a horrible mess we're in now.' I said, Horrible, yes, all wars were horrible: but mess, no. 'Oh, of course,' she said, 'we can't possibly lose, or anything like that. But I'm afraid I was thinking of you and me, my dear Caroline. The last war marked the end of our childhood: this one will mark the end of our youth.' This sounded so neat that I mistrusted it: neat things are hardly ever quite true. It is pure nonsense, of course. One can't, thank goodness, divide one's life into watertight compartments like that.

She finished up by saying, lugubriously, 'Of course, even if the war turns out all right the world is never going to be quite the same again.' I have now had this remark made to me by at least a dozen different people, and it baffles me more every time I hear it. What on earth, I wonder, does it mean? If it was made by people who had a husband or son in danger, one could understand it only too well. But it isn't. Those ones, mostly, don't discuss the future at all; they just live in the present, as though it was a little circle of lamplight in a dark room. No, the people who talk like this all seem to be the ones who have nothing more precious to lose than a sense of material security and a comfortable certainty that while they are down at dinner a well-trained housemaid will go into the drawing-room and plump up the cushions. They make me sick and tired. 'The world is never going to be quite the same' – good heavens, has it been such a grand world up till now (except for a few lucky ones like ourselves) that one should try to keep it unchanged? Have we any right to grumble if our lights go from green to red and the other stream of traffic gets a turn?

Besides, everything that really matters always does go on being the same: the fun of thinking things out, and delight in awareness for its own sake, and, above all, the unending fascination of personal relationships. To say nothing of such trifles as love and courage and kindness and integrity and the quite astonishing resilience of the human spirit. War may crack the individual records, but it can't destroy the matrix of things like these. However, although one can write all this down in a letter, one really cannot embark on it to Agnes over a cup of coffee in Sloane Street at 11 o'clock in the morning. So I just said vaguely, No, I supposed not. She sighed, and added with a sense of personal grievance, 'It does seem a little hard, I must say, that one should have been unlucky enough to live in a time like this.'

Good old Agnes, how she clarifies one's thoughts for one. Till that moment I had not realized how passionately I felt that I would not live in any other time if you paid me. I didn't say so; after all, the coffee was on her. But when I left her I found myself crossing the street with particular care, because it would be so awful to get run over just now and not be there to see what was going to happen.

With love, yours ever,

Caroline.

Time-Lag Tragedies

20th December 1939

Dearest Susan,

Thank you for your letter, or rather your protest. All right,
I apologize – not for what I actually said about Agnes
Lingfield in my last letter, but for what I didn't bother to say.
That is the worst of letters, even long ones. So often, one has
just enough time to describe some mood or incident in detail,
but not enough to sketch in the background without which its
proper values are lost.

You scold me for saying, apropos of Agnes's lamentations,
that 'everything that really matters will go on being the same,'
war or no war. That's all very well, you say, but what about
the thousands of people who were already having a struggle
to make ends meet, and who are now completely ruined?
What, for instance, about your and Clem's old governess,
who has invested every penny of her savings in her West
Kensington boarding-house and whose lodgers have all van-
ished to the country? You say you doubt whether 'the fun of
thinking things out' and 'delight in awareness for its own
sake' will be much consolation to *her*. My dearest woman, I
had not forgotten about Miss Baines (as a matter of fact I
went to see her last week – but I'll tell you about that later).
Nor had I forgotten about all the other unadvertised tragedies

which the outgoing tide has left behind it in big cities – the small bookseller, the small upholsterer, the garage proprietor, the man who sells old prints, the woman who sells home-made cakes. One couldn't possibly forget about these people: they make up, so far, the war's biggest casualty list – and they haven't even got the consolations of glory.

In moments of sane detachment one can see that we are living simultaneously through a war and a revolution; and that – provided we can win the war quickly enough – the world which we are going to build up out of the revolution has got to be a world in which this kind of distress doesn't arise. But one can't expect people to look at the long view when they are being forced to focus all their attention on wobbly stepping-stones in order to save themselves from drowning. The fact that they are, so to speak, time-lag tragedies doesn't make them any less tragic.

These real victims were exactly the background against which I meant you to see my picture of Agnes Lingfield wailing and bleating that nothing was ever going to be the same again – when all she meant was that she might have to order two courses instead of four and put away everything except the 'flat' silver. The other people, astoundingly and to their eternal credit, don't wail. They have too much pride: and besides, never having got into the habit of leaning too heavily on a sense of security, they don't entirely lose their balance when it is removed. Whereas Agnes is like one of those drapy droopy elegant women in 18th-century pictures: you've only got to twitch the marble-and-ormolu pedestal from under her elbow and there she lies sprawling.

But actually, even if I had been talking about the real tragedies instead of the bogus ones, I still shouldn't take back what I said. 'Delight in noticing things,' and so on, may not, as you say, be *much* consolation when your savings are lost and your home broken up; but to most people it is a little consolation, and a little is better than none. A bankrupt boarding-house keeper who enjoys watching trees come out

in Kensington Gardens is just that much happier, you can't
deny, than a bankrupt boarding-house keeper who doesn't. As
a matter of fact, Miss Baines said something very like this
when I went to see her. She was showing me her bowls of
bulbs.

'I'm so glad I found time to get those planted,' she said. 'I
was almost too busy to do it before war broke out; and now
they're one of the few things that keep me going. Look – I've
planted a measuring stick in each bowl; it makes something to
come downstairs for every morning. And another thing,' she
said, 'I often think, especially in the evenings, how glad I am
I made all the children I was with learn such a lot of poetry
by heart. I don't know whether Clem and Susan have
remembered any of it, but *I* have. And I keep on thinking,
well, that's *one* lodger that can't give me notice, anyhow.'
(This reminded me of a remark that Badger made right at the
beginning of the war, when it looked as though we were going
to get no plays, films, pictures, or music at all. 'We must live
on stored beauty,' he said, 'like a squirrel on nuts.')

I've asked Miss Baines down to Starlings for Christmas. If
Clem gets leave she will love to see him again, and even if he
doesn't she says she'll enjoy being in a house full of children.
On the spur of the moment it was the only way I could think
of to cheer her up; but I know perfectly well that this kind of
thing doesn't solve the eventual problem of Miss B., or of all
the other Miss B.s. Which brings one back to the old argument between the Lady Bountiful and the Impatient
Revolutionary, as to whether it's worth while patching up a
dilapidated house – or social system, or world order, or whatever you like – when what is really needed is a new one. The
L.B. sends a nice bowl of soup to the poor, and then sits back
and thinks she's done the whole of her duty. The I.R., with a
sneer of 'Palliatives!', rushes off to recognize the world, and
thinks he's doing the whole of *his*. Personally, I believe
they're both wrong. It certainly isn't enough to send soup
and then think no more about it: but it equally isn't enough to

reform the world (which can't be done in a flash) and leave people, in the meanwhile, soupless.

The truth is, some of us are more suited by nature to be Palliators, or Patchers, and others to be Rebuilders; very few have either the time or the temperament to do both jobs. There ought to be some arrangement by which all the people who are trying to clear up the present mess could label themselves either 'P' or 'R,' and guarantee not to interfere with each other's jobs while continuing to get on with their own. That would enable half of them to go on providing the necessary soup until the other half had finished creating the much better world in which charity soup won't be needed. To make out that these two methods can't be used concurrently seems to me dangerous nonsense.

What a dissertation . . . But if you will go and accuse me of being callous about Miss Baines, just because I am (quite unrepentantly) brutal about Agnes, you bring it on yourself!—

With love, yours ever,

Caroline.

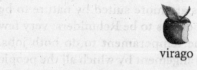

virago

To buy any of our books and to find out more
about Virago Press and Virago Modern Classics,
our authors and titles, as well as events and
book club forum, visit our websites

www.virago.co.uk
www.littlebrown.co.uk

and follow us on Twitter

@ViragoBooks

To order any Virago titles p & p free in the UK,
please contact our mail order supplier on:

+ 44 (0)1832 737525

Customers not based in the UK should contact
the same number for appropriate postage
and packing costs.